Seeing the City with the Eyes of God

Floyd McClung

Published by
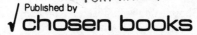
chosen books

FLEMING H. REVELL COMPANY
TARRYTOWN, NEW YORK

Library of Congress Cataloging-in-Publication Data

McClung, Floyd.
    [Spirits of the city]
    Seeing cities with the eyes of God / Floyd McClung.
      p.   cm.
    Original British ed. published under title: The spirits of the city.
    ISBN 0-8007-9177-0
    1. Cities and towns—Religious aspects—Christianity. 2. City churches. I. Title.
    BR115.C45M34 1991
    270.8′2′091732—dc20   90-23487
                                                 CIP

A Chosen book
Copyright © 1991 by Floyd McClung

Chosen Books Publishing Company, Ltd.
Published by
Fleming H. Revell Company
Tarrytown, New York
Printed in the United States of America

This book is dedicated to
all my fellow YWAMers
who have committed
their lives to making the welfare
of the city their welfare.
May God grant you grace for the task.

Contents

Foreword
A Tale of Many Cities...

It is the greatest mass migration in human history, and it will touch the lives of every person on this planet. The explosion of large, multi-million-person cities is radically affecting economic and political policies. Some cities are industrial centers that attract hundreds of thousands of people hoping for employment. Others are cultural and education centers, luring the youth of a nation. Still others function as seats of national and regional governments and, therefore, control the distribution of power and wealth in a nation.

There is no escaping the influence and power of the city. It has become the dominant social force in the world. Cities are the mountain peaks of society; trends, ideologies and fashions are born in the fermenting cauldron of city life and then flow down and out to influence the populace.

What is the Christian response to the city? Are we to see her as a threat to a secure and comfortable lifestyle? Are we to avoid the city as a stronghold of evil? Should we do all in our power to avoid the city lest we be endangered or contaminated by her inhabitants?

Surely a theological understanding of the city is needed, one that is rooted firmly in biblical truth: We must look in God's Word for our responses. No other approach is sufficient for the truly committed Christian.

Understanding God's sovereign purposes for the city is essential if believers are to have the inspiration and faith necessary to respond to today's urban challenges—unemployment, divorce, homelessness, alcohol-related emergencies, racial inequality and tension.

Cities are magnets for the runaway, throwaway kids who cannot or will not live in homes where they are molested, beaten and rejected. Increasingly, orphanages are filling with kids whose parents are alive but simply don't want them.

A crucial test of the moral character of a society is found in how it treats its outcasts. Modern Western societies will be judged all the more harshly, not only because of how we treat our children, but because of the way we created their wounds. Never before have nations had so much wealth and so little compassion.

The Bible begins in a garden but ends in a city. God's redemptive purposes for every person include a community of believers who love and accept him, and show the way to God's forgiveness. The heavenly city of God in the book of Revelation points to a way of life that must begin in the earthly city of man. To turn our backs on the city is to turn away from God's eternal purposes of salvation and justice for His whole creation. To accept this challenge is to embrace God's call to seek the *shalom* of the city. Blessed are the peacemakers. . . .

Part 1
The Fight for the City

1
The Powers at Work

The incredulous look on the face of the farmer-turned-city-dweller said it all. His incredulity turned into a smile, almost laughter, as he settled down to hear me out. His resistance to what I was saying made it hard for me to concentrate. I was speaking to a group of suburban Christians and sharing a biblical view of cities that they obviously found hard to believe.

"The city is God's idea," I declared. "When He created Adam and Eve, He intended for them to have children and populate Eden."

Watching the dubious looks on their faces, I carried on. "When we think of a city we have images in our minds that are primarily negative, based on news reports of gang violence, drug wars, unemployed youth and homeless people. But try to imagine what the Garden would have been like without sin. What if Adam and Eve had obeyed God?"

I tried to help my audience imagine the Garden of Eden without the Fall. If all the inhabitants had obeyed God and had supervised the natural resources at their disposal creatively and unselfishly, what would have been the result? What kind of community would have developed had there been unity and harmony in their relationships and social interactions? As they grew in number a small city would have emerged, different from anything we know today.

When we think of cities we picture scenes of humanity crowded into urban slum areas and inner-city ghettos. We think of size—massive numbers of people and massive problems. But to put these problems into biblical perspective we must remember that God's original plan had to do with community, a covenant people gathered in a place to serve Him. Without this understanding we will view modern-day "city gatherings" negatively, based on the problems we see at hand. To understand the city biblically we must go back to God's original intention for mankind. Without this basis, we will have at best an incomplete view of the city, and at worst a warped and destructive theology of the city that leads to the total abandonment of the urban world.

The need for a theology for the city is urgent. A belief that cities are inherently evil will affect not only our attitudes toward the city, but also our understanding of the role of the Church in modern society. Though the Church should have developed an urban theology long ago out of a desire to understand God's mandate to "multiply and fill the earth," we are now *forced* to respond because of the urbanization of our planet. Cities can no longer be ignored.

Most definitions of the city are based, unfortunately, on sociological interpretations of the city's function. While it is helpful to understand this perspective, it is more important to understand God's purpose in creating mankind with a longing for city "togetherness."

A Christian leader once commented to me, "God created the earth, but it was man who made the city. It was the consequence of his rebellion against God that led Cain to start the first city. This was a way of building his own society, showing that he did not need or want God. And that's how it's been ever since. Cities are the collecting places for sinful humanity and all our problems. Now Satan rules the cities because of man's sin." This is not an isolated view and, consequently, it is no wonder that the Church has had so little impact on the city.

I found out later that the farmer I mentioned at the beginning had lost everything he owned in a drought and was forced to find employment in a nearby city. He felt, on the one hand, that God had used his need for a job to bring him to the city, but he felt, on the other hand, that the city was without hope and doomed to destruction. He tried to love the people around him, but felt he was in enemy territory.

Many Christians live with this tension, feeling obligated to love the city but disliking it deeply. This tension has led some believers to spiritualize their reactions in order to justify their rejection of the city. They have developed a theology of escape, a view that says God is against the city and it is under His judgment. They see the city as a form of institutional evil. They have failed not only to seek out God's views on bringing people to the city, but to respond with His love for the city dweller.

Just like the individuals who inhabit them, cities are fallen. Though they take on a life and power of their own, a city is people, a group of individuals. They have worth and value to God both as individuals *and as a community*. Just as we have learned individually that we are significant and valuable to the Lord even though we have sinned against Him, so whole communities have a place in God's plan. Just as we have learned that it is important to love the neediest person because he is created in God's image, so we must learn to love the neediest city for the same reason.

Without a biblical theology of the city we will succumb to the prevailing pessimism around us. We will develop a hopelessness that will undermine our love and faith for the city. A state of unbelief toward the city already permeates the Church, and obviously undercuts our mandate to be salt and light in society.

God intends the Church to have a role of moral and spiritual leadership in modern society. If the primary attitude toward the city is negative, how can the Church provide such leadership, located outside the city itself? You cannot effectively lead someone you do not like; the very nature of spiritual leadership is based on love and relationship.

The most powerful influence the Church can have on society is through prayer. But without a biblical perspective on the city, our prayers will be filled with unbelief.

Obviously we will never develop a personal love for the city if we believe it is inherently evil. Without a change of theology concerning the city we will continue to hold our suburban and rural lifestyles as sacrosanct. We will rationalize our flight from the city with pious concerns about our family, when all the time our real motivation was fear and selfishness.

We will explore God's purpose and plan for the city in later chapters, but let's look first at the idea of evil in the city. If it is not inherent, where does it come from? To find the solution, it will help to understand the cause.

Spiritual Warfare

There is a personal evil being called Satan. He tempted Jesus, put betrayal into the heart of Judas, sought to deceive Peter, filled the heart of Ananias with lies, prowls around like a lion seeking to destroy believers, and is sometimes disguised as an angel of light (Matthew 4:1; 16:23; John 13:2; 1 Peter 5:8; Acts 5:3; 2 Corinthians 2:11).

All Bible-believing Christians acknowledge the reality of Satan. Spiritual warfare is also a reality. It is the nature of that warfare that raises questions. Perhaps one of Satan's greatest tactics in attacking God's people is to intimidate us into silence on this subject. We are concerned about extremism. We have learned that if we leave well enough alone, we won't stir up problems. At least, that is what we like to think will happen.

If indeed there is a fallen spiritual being called Satan, and he heads a host of demons who are warring against the saints, then it is the greatest of all follies to ignore this warfare or treat it lightly.

I have not always understood this. I remember speaking to a group of university students in New Zealand in 1977. One of them asked me about my beliefs concerning the devil and spiritual warfare. I said, "Satan loves sin, fear and attention, and I will not give him any of the three. Next question, please." I thought by refusing to give time even to discuss the matter that I was treating the question in an appropriate manner.

Later that night, when I was alone and had time to reflect on the events of the day, I experienced a deep sense of sorrow. I did not understand what I had done wrong, but I felt that somehow I had grieved the Holy Spirit during the course of the day. I bowed in prayer and asked the Lord what was wrong. My answer to the student's question earlier in the day came to mind. A quiet voice within me said, *I am disappointed in your response. You have little knowledge of the demonic realm and no authority over Satan as did My disciples many years ago. Your answer reflected your own fears.*

It hit me that I really knew nothing firsthand about spiritual warfare; much less was I available to the Lord to set a needy person free of demonic bondage. The words the Lord spoke to me that night pierced my soul. I had no spiritual authority in this area. What was elementary in the discipleship training of the early followers of Jesus was a great void in my own life. I was responding in fear—a well-disguised fear dressed up in theological terms, but fear nevertheless. It may have fooled some people, but not the Lord. I was afraid of extremism. I was afraid of the unknown.

The fact that there were people in need who could not be helped because of my spiritual impotence bothered me greatly. That night years ago in New Zealand I read the words of Jesus from Matthew 10:1: "And he called to him his twelve disciples and gave them authority over unclean spirits, to cast them out. . . ." I asked Him to teach me about spiritual warfare. I asked Him for spiritual authority over unclean spirits. I prayed a simple prayer and asked the Lord Jesus to take away my fear and to give me authority just as He had given it to His disciples many years ago.

That prayer put me in a frame of mind to learn. Nothing dramatic or emotional happened to me, but I started studying God's Word to find out everything it said about demons and spiritual powers. I wanted to know how Satan attacked people. In the process of studying the Scriptures, I discovered not only that the devil has tactics that fall into recognizable patterns, but that God has given Christians spiritual armor to defend themselves against the attacks of the enemy.

Spiritual Warfare in the City

What exactly does spiritual warfare have to do with cities? Any Christian who lives or works in a city—whether suburbs or inner city—without taking seriously the warfare that exists there is in for big problems. I am amazed that so many Christians are so ignorant of the spiritual battle that is being fought all around them.

In fact, I am astounded that so little is written or taught about this subject by evangelical Christians. I can find only two books addressing the topic of spiritual warfare as it relates to the Church's role in the city, *The Meaning of the City* by Jacques Ellul and *Taking Our Cities for God* by John Dawson.

This lack of attention must cause us to wonder: Are we losing our cities to immorality because we are ignorant of the spiritual battles being fought over them? Have we fallen prey unwittingly to the devices of Satan? Are we bereft of the spiritual weapons at our disposal? Have whole ministries been defeated and churches divided because of Satan? Are the families of spiritual leaders and pastors being targeted by the enemy? I am convinced that the answer to these questions is yes. Over and over again, yes.

Further, when we observe the superficial nature of Western culture and its bent toward self-realization, leisure, compulsive spending, apolitical passivity and moral permissiveness, we have to question the role of the demonic in the decline of Christian character. Around the turn of the century a fundamental cultural transformation occurred. Prior to this time, our culture was oriented to the importance of work, savings, Christian morality, the nuclear family and even self-denial. Liberal Protestantism, the death of absolutes, the emergence of a therapeutic ethos among the educated in society, and national marketing forces all coalesced to encourage this cultural transformation. While it is easy to oversimplify the suddenness or completeness of the changes that took place in society, the resulting consumer culture is not. It is pervasive.

The erosion of Christian morality in every sphere of life is not just the result of the denial of biblical absolutes. I contend that spiritual powers are always at work when evil is present. Satan is called the prince of the power of the air. When people are disobedient, follow the passions of the flesh and are by nature filled with wrath, their state is associated with Satan's influence (Ephesians 2:2). There is a difference between the temporal, or the seen, and the spiritual and unseen.

This is illustrated in the Greek tragedies. While the mortals acted on one level of the stage, the "gods" acted on another. The audience saw a split-level stage with two simultaneous plays, totally interrelated but visually distinct. Likewise, the spiritual realm is unseen but real, intertwined with the lives of ordinary men and women.

When people are slaves to their passions, they are described in the Bible as "foolish, disobedient, led astray" (Titus 3:3). The Bible attributes this state of fallenness and depravity to having their minds blinded by "the god of this world" (2 Corinthians 4:4).

Culture is influenced directly by spiritual forces. This has a great effect on Christians. Leaders fall into immorality, financial problems develop and good people turn against each other. Whole churches are being defeated and divided because of our ignorance and fear concerning spiritual warfare.

We know there are many challenges facing those who live in the city, and we will look at some of these in later chapters, but first we need to acknowledge that there is another dynamic at work besides the natural pressures and temptations that result from living in a fallen world. Why are there so many problems for Christians in the city? Are the problems people face there more than just the need to adjust to the faster-paced life? I suggest that these problems are not just the inevitable result of living in a busy city, but are also part of Satan's effort to defeat God's people.

We must also consider the social problems of the city in the context of spiritual warfare: poverty, unemployment, prostitution, loneliness, chemical dependency, gang violence, abandoned and abused children, homelessness and AIDS. How do all these relate to spiritual powers at work in the city? Is Satan seeking to destroy whole people groups? Does he exploit weaknesses, using people's sins and the sins committed against them as a platform from which to bring them under bondage?

We recognize that the world's greatest problem is sin. But if we ignore or downplay Satan's role in attacking and destroying people's lives, we are missing what God's Word teaches us. Adam and Eve were punished because they disobeyed God, but Satan played a strategic role in tempting them. In the same way he will tempt people today.

The Bible says that "we are not contending against flesh and blood, but against the principalities, against the powers, against the world rulers of this present darkness, against the spiritual hosts of wickedness in the heavenly places" (Ephesians 6:12). God's Word is clear: Demonic powers are at work in the world; believers are engaged in spiritual warfare. While we can envisage spiritism and the occult quite easily in non-Western nations, we have yet to take seriously spiritual warfare in our own country.

Demonic powers attack individuals, groups, institutions, structures and social mores in the city. Satan's tactics in harassing people are described throughout the Scriptures. He attacks in order to bring people into bondage to sin and the flesh. He tries to discourage them emotionally in order to defeat them spiritually. He will use any means at his disposal, and he will not ask permission first.

Satan can do only what the Lord allows (Job 1:6–12), but sin in our lives does give him a platform to harass and tempt us (Romans 1:18–25; Ephesians 2:1–3). He attacks us physically (2 Corinthians 12:7; Matthew 9:32–33; 12:22), morally (2 Corinthians 2:11) and in our thought lives (Matthew 4:10; 16:22–23; Acts 5:3).

Satan seeks to lead the Church into error; thus, we are warned to "test the spirits" (1 John 4:1–3). James also admonishes the Church that there is an earthly wisdom that is "devilish" (James 3:15). Paul foretells a day when teaching will be introduced into the Church at the instigation of evil spirits (1 Timothy 4:1).

Satan has an advantage over many believers because of a great ignorance on our part of the power and reality of demonic deception, and because of our general incomprehension of the principles of biblical demonology.

The Powers

The apostle Paul refers repeatedly to the fact that spiritual entities influence events in the life of the Church. He uses a number of terms to describe the forces or beings at work, as we read in the following verses, but I would like to focus on one: the word *powers* as it relates to the subject of spiritual warfare with Satan for the city.

Regarding the other terms Paul uses—*principalities, powers, rulers, dominions, authorities*—Hendrik Berkhof suggests that since Paul never gives distinct meanings to them, it is not necessary for us to do so in order to understand his message (*Christ and the Powers*, p. 15). It is important to note, however, that, in the context, Paul makes abundantly clear the *general* meaning he has for them.

> For I am sure that neither death, nor life, nor angels, nor principalities, nor things present, nor things to come, nor powers, nor height, nor depth, nor anything else in all creation, will be able to separate us from the love of God in Christ Jesus our Lord.
>
> Romans 8:38–39

Then comes the end, when he delivers the kingdom to God the Father after destroying every rule and every authority and power. For he must reign until he has put all his enemies under his feet.

1 Corinthians 15:24–25

[God] raised [Jesus] from the dead and made him sit at his right hand in the heavenly places, far above all rule and authority and power and dominion.

Ephesians 1:20–21

. . .you once walked, following the course of this world, following the prince of the power of the air, the spirit that is now at work in the sons of disobedience.

Ephesians 2:2

Through the church the manifold wisdom of God might now be made known to the principalities and powers in the heavenly places.

Ephesians 3:10

For we are not contending against flesh and blood, but against the principalities, against the powers, against the world rulers of this present darkness, against the spiritual hosts of wickedness in the heavenly places.

Ephesians 6:12

In him all things were created, in heaven and on earth, visible and invisible, whether thrones or dominions or principalities or authorities [powers].

Colossians 1:16

> He disarmed the principalities and powers and made a
> public example of them, triumphing over them in him.
>
> Colossians 2:15

We draw several vital conclusions by examining these passages:

1. *The powers are created by Christ.*

Paul does not hesitate to declare that all things were created "through him and for him," even though they are not now fulfilling the purpose for which they were created.

2. *They are personal spiritual beings.*

Paul attributes the faculties and volition of reason to the powers (1 Corinthians 2:8). Further, he speaks of Christ's disarming the powers and making a public example of them (Colossians 2:15). Something impersonal would not need to be disarmed and humiliated. Though Paul names the powers as distinct from the angels in Romans 8:38, this does not preclude the possibility that the powers are fallen angels.

3. *They influence events on earth.*

Not only do they seek to lead humankind into all sorts of evil (Ephesians 2:2) but they also participated in the crucifixion of the Lord Jesus (1 Corinthians 2:8).

4. *The function of the powers is to seek domination, primarily through religious means, over God's creation.*

Paul stresses the relationship between the powers and their desire to dominate God's creation in Colossians 2:8, 14, 18: "See to it that no one makes a prey of you. . . . [God has canceled] the bond which stood against us. . . . Let no one disqualify you."

The structures, religious traditions and philosophy referred to here are not the powers, but the way the powers rule over people. In a similar passage, Paul says that while he was under the law, he was a slave to the elemental spirits of the universe (Galatians 4:1–3), reinforcing his teaching that the powers use religious means to dominate people.

5. *If the powers cannot control people through religious means, they will exploit human passions and desires.*

Paul tells Titus that until the goodness and lovingkindness of God our Savior appeared, we were "foolish, disobedient, *led astray,* slaves to various passions and pleasures" (Titus 3:3, italics mine). He further names Satan as the one working to lead us to live by the passions of our flesh (Ephesians 2:2–3).

6. *The powers are evil.*

What other conclusion can we reach about the powers since they crucified Christ, deceive mankind, exploit the passions of humanity and use religion to dominate millions of people? Though not the devil's *invention* (he is a created being and can create nothing), the powers are certainly vulnerable to the devil's *intention.*

7. *The domination the powers held over God's creation was exposed and defeated at the cross.*

Paul declares triumphantly that Christ "disarmed the principalities and powers and made a public example of them, triumphing over them in him" (Colossians 2:15). Why then do the powers continue to harass believers? Defeated but not destroyed is the answer—just as the Nazis were defeated on D-Day in World War II, but still fought until V-Day many months later.

The exposure of the powers at the cross is central to their defeat, for their hold on people is based on a lie. Part of their hold is rooted in the lie that they are all-powerful and worthy of devotion. Through Christ's death and resurrection this lie is made public for all to see.

Dethroning the Powers

The powers are defeated, but when the Kingdom of God is proclaimed, they react; they attack those who proclaim the Good News viciously. In fact, the very act of declaring that Christ died and rose again is a declaration of war.

The presence of Christians reminds the powers that they are defeated. The presence of the Church shakes Satan's kingdom; holy men and women are public witness to his lies. By her faith and life the Church exposes Satan's powerlessness and his ultimate and final destruction.

Because of this Satan retaliates. His weapons are fashioned from deceit, pride and fear. He will use every tactic possible to stop believers from hindering his work.

At the same time, whenever Christ is proclaimed, a limit is set on the ability of the powers to deceive and dominate. Not ignorant of his devices, we lean on Jesus and His victory. We refuse to be impressed with Satan's ways, realizing that when he is most frightened he makes the greatest effort to stop us. Nevertheless, we seek to discern the powers in order to withstand them and see them defeated as we lift up the conquering Christ.

In the cities our warfare is just beginning.

2
Discerning the Spirits of the City

Through my experience of working in cities I have come to believe that certain kinds of demonic powers are prevalent in certain places, depending on the sins that have given Satan a spiritual beachhead. John the apostle mentions Satan's throne in Pergamum (Revelation 2:12–13), for example. Whether John was referring to local religious practices, or meant Satan had established his rule in that place, we do not know. What is important to learn from this passage is the localized nature of Satan's presence. It is essential that we recognize and respond to those demons peculiar to the city we live in.

Demonic bondage is normally associated with individuals, but the moral disintegration of our society makes the possibility of large-scale spiritual warfare against entire cities or nations seem possible. The Greek word used for principalities is *archa*, which is variously translated as beginnings, origins, rulers, authorities and rule. Bauer, Arndt and Gingrich say this word is used to refer to "angelic and demonic powers, since they were thought of as having a political organization" (*A Greek-English Lexicon of the New Testament*, p. 112). Concerning the term *world rulers* used by Paul in Ephesians 6:12, they say it refers in part to spirit beings who were thought of as having parts of the cosmos under their control.

That Paul uses the words *principalities, powers* and *world rulers* in the context of "this present darkness" (Ephesians 6:12) seems to point to his understanding of a hierarchy in the demonic realm that has been assigned to specific places and tasks. Paul uses the Greek word *exousias,* and it is interesting to note, as the *Lexicon* points out, that this word is used elsewhere to refer to rulers and those to whom they have delegated their power.

This is consistent with Daniel's reference to the "prince of Persia," a spiritual being who opposed the angel of the Lord (Daniel 10:10–14). The angel said that the "prince of the kingdom of Persia" had withstood him for days in his attempt to come to Daniel. Evidently a demonic power or principality was assigned by Satan to rule over his interest in Persia. This demonic being warred against the angel of the Lord because he recognized in Daniel an important adversary. If Daniel's prayers were answered, Satan's cause would be dealt a great defeat, so the battle was on.

The Scriptures say very little about the nature and names of demon powers, so we must be cautious about naming spirits over places. We can, however, recognize evil in the systems, institutions and lives of people in the city, and how that evil spirit manifests itself. Because of the association of evil and the demonic in Scripture, we may refer to the "spirit of greed" or "the spirit of violence" or whatever evil spiritual power seems to be manifesting itself in unusual dimensions in a city or nation.

If we have a view of sin that is limited to personal choices, we will miss an important truth: Cities and nations take on spiritual characters and lives of their own. This corporate spiritual character is potentially good or evil, dependent on the response of the people to God or Satan.

Further, it is vital to recognize that principalities and demonic powers seek to use wickedness in a city as a launching pad to attack Christians. It is essential that we do not enter the "battle arena" without arming ourselves with the full armor of God. It is foolish to attempt God's work without a sufficient prayer base and an understanding of the spiritual weapons at our disposal.

Moreover, God has raised up prophets in the Church, some of them in the form of sociologists and theologians to "discern the spirits" and alert the Church to the presence of evil in political and economic institutions and society in general.

I am deeply troubled by the narrow view of spiritual warfare held by many Christians. God has given us prophets to warn the Church, but their words are often not taken seriously. If ever the Church needs to hear her prophets, it is now.

Discerning spiritual attacks and heeding warnings give one insight on how to respond to difficult situations. My wife, Sally, and I led a team in the red-light district of Amsterdam for several years. For the first few years every woman on our team who lived in the neighborhood experienced some form of depression. After fasting and prayer, we became convinced that this was a spiritual attack to discourage our workers and close down our ministry of evangelism among the prostitutes.

We believed we had discerned a particular enemy attack on our workers and prayed against a spirit of depression.

After many days of prayer the attack was broken. God gave us a new level of spiritual authority to withstand the attacks. Although the victory was the Lord's, we learned that He was using the situation to teach us principles of spiritual warfare.

God wanted us, first, to *discern* that a spiritual attack went beyond natural explanations for why people were suffering. Then He could show us how to respond, corporately and individually. God wanted us, second, to *teach* our staff from His Word how to discern and react to the lies of the enemy and his attacks on their minds and emotions. Sally calls this "developing practical weapons for spiritual warfare." We must act in practical obedience to God's Word, putting into practice scriptural principles that arm us with righteousness and protection in each situation we face. We will look more at these principles in the next chapter.

Discerning Principalities and Powers

Sin gives Satan a platform to attack people. Corporate sin in the life of a city also gives Satan a foothold over the city or institutions within it. After visiting scores of cities on every continent, I am convinced there are some principalities that are common to all cities, and some that are peculiar to particular ones. The spirit of greed at work in Monte Carlo and Las Vegas is unusual in its proportions, as is the spirit of sexual immorality in San Francisco and Amsterdam. Many people comment about the spirit of power at work in Washington, D.C., and how many good men and women have been blind to its work and thus fallen prey to its deceptive grip.

Violence, anger, loneliness and sensuality seem to be more than human problems in many cities. Satan uses sin to gain a foothold, and then he drives people to extremes, often beyond what they want themselves.

How do we discern when spiritual powers are at work? We look for obsession with particular sins and an unusual "drivenness" toward evil in an entire population. It is important to watch for monolithic deception in a city, particularly in basic areas of morality. When a whole population is being destroyed, it should put us on the alert, no matter what the natural causes. We must also be on the lookout for an "antichrist" spirit, when Christians are despised in an almost irrational manner.

There are four important characteristics helpful in discerning the work of principalities and powers on a broad scale in cities and nations: spiritual blindness and hardness toward the Gospel; obsession with certain forms of evil throughout vast portions of the population; bondage to particular sins and behavior that cannot be controlled by normal means used by societies to govern themselves; and compromise and defeat in the Church (Romans 1:18–32).

Satan often uses the problems of a city as an opportunity to introduce false solutions. The drive to accomplish—even in the area of recreation—has produced an incredible amount of impersonalness. People are "busier" having fun, so busy they have to work harder to pay for all they are doing, and move faster to get it all done.

Has technology made our "highly developed" Western nations more humane, more moral? On the contrary, the soul of the consumer machine is sick. We live increasingly isolated, lonely lives. We try to comfort ourselves with our machines and appliances, satiated with the best stereo sound, fed with food zapped in microwave ovens and overwhelmed with channels to watch on our cable-fed TVs, direct from satellites circling quietly above us.

Then the enemy of our souls comes along and says, "Life can be much better. I have just the thing for you. You are living too fast. Slow down. Discover yourself. Look at the crystal rock, meditate and chant after me. . . ."

Exercising the gift of discernment of spirits is crucial. We must know if we are battling demonic powers or dealing just with sin and its consequences in the culture. The two are not always the same. Further, if the battle is against demonic powers, what kinds of powers are we fighting? It is important to know the exact kinds of strategies Satan is using, and how they got rooted in the culture. I have found that a relationship usually exists between demonic bondage in a city or nation and the sins that have been committed there on a large scale in the past. Sometimes we have to go back centuries to find the roots of some spiritual bondages.

Some years ago I was in Norway for a time of extended ministry and I preached in several cities. After my meetings I was usually available to talk with people if they had questions. Over and over again I was amazed at how many people were struggling with deep, life-controlling fears. This pattern was so widespread that I began to ask ministers and friends if this was a common problem. They all agreed that it was.

I was puzzled about this, until a friend mentioned in passing that Christianity was introduced in Norway through a king in the eleventh century. He marched through the country with his army, putting to death all the citizens of the land who refused to become Christians. Christianity was born there in a national bloodbath.

I am convinced that events such as these have a profound spiritual impact on a nation. Satan takes advantage of this kind of national trauma, and seeks to use it to establish spiritual strongholds. Principalities begin to work, and will not be driven out until they are recognized and the appropriate steps are taken to deliver the nation from the attack of these demonic powers against the people.

3
Power Encounters

The very existence of spiritual powers raises tough issues for us that must be addressed. What is to be our response to the presence of demonic powers?

We know we are given authority as believers to stand against spiritual powers of darkness because of the victory won for us on the cross by the Lord Jesus, but does that mean Christians should aggressively challenge the strongholds of Satan embedded in institutions and political systems in our cities?

This question implies a further question, and that is: Who is the lord of society? On the one hand, we realize that society and culture are God's gifts to us. He has created us as social beings, placed us on earth with stewardship over its resources, made us to interact with others and to live in human community, and established government to bring order and peace in nations. Because God is the creator of all things and the ruler of this universe, we may take for granted that His purpose is for righteousness to rule in the earth. The earth is the Lord's.

Although society is the Lord's, it is now also Satan's. It was the devil who offered Jesus the nations of this world when he tempted Him in the desert. We recognize the reality of the kingdom of darkness and that man has fallen prey to Satan's evil devices. Culture does not often reflect the glory of God; it is fallen just as man is fallen.

We can take heart from Jesus' temptation in the wilderness. Though Satan promised Jesus everything, the Lord resisted his offer and overcame him. He went on to defeat him at the cross—Satan's shame was made public for all to see. The temptation in the wilderness is a drama now being played again. What Satan failed to accomplish in the heart of the Lord Jesus he now seeks to establish in the hearts of those who follow Jesus. We are engaged in a spiritual conflict, the outcome of which will determine who has the spiritual leadership in our world. The outcome of that first temptation is our assurance of the outcome of the second, if we fulfill the conditions put before us for victory over the enemy.

Just as victory was won in the wilderness through the exercise of spiritual authority by the Lord Jesus, we must challenge the lies Satan is hurling at the world today. He has strongholds, but they are vulnerable to those who come against them armed for war.

The Weapons of Our Warfare

Our primary weapons against Satan start on a personal level and extend to the corporate warfare of the Church and her role in society. In the following pages we will discuss seven categories of spiritual weapons. Each category is related to the others and together they form a spiritual armor that allows the Church not only to exist but to triumph over evil in society.

Inner Reality with God

Spiritual warfare can never be divorced from the basics of trusting in the Lord Jesus Christ for salvation, living a holy life, applying God's Word and God's character to our business dealings and relationships, fellowshiping with other believers, reading the Scriptures daily and being filled with the Holy Spirit. The spiritual armor for the believer that is described in Ephesians 6 speaks to the importance of a right relationship with the Lord and others. Unless our minds are protected with the helmet of salvation, our hearts covered with the breastplate of righteousness, our innermost beings girded with truth, our feet prepared to bring the Gospel of peace to others, and unless we hold up the shield of faith with which we quench the accusations and attacks of the enemy, we are vulnerable.

There is no substitute for personal foundations of righteousness, servanthood, teachableness and hunger for God. If we do not cultivate these spiritual passions, carnal passions will dominate and control us. Unless we have inner reality with God, we will be overcome by other "realities." If individuals are vulnerable the whole Church is vulnerable: A weak Church will not be able to play the role destined for it by God in society.

Though intimacy with God is the foundation for personal spiritual growth, we sometimes look mistakenly for inner reality in ourselves. Sin has always been built on the claim that we have a right to our own lives, along with the notion that we have a right to see things from our own point of view. Though it sounds quite pious and acceptable to say that religion is a "personal thing," it is not true.

Modern individualism has so infiltrated the thinking of Western believers that we confuse the priesthood of the believer with a selfish form of Christianity and, thus, have isolated Christians in a kind of privatistic Christianity. The consequences are selfishness in lifestyle and a compromise of intellectual integrity. Our credibility and spiritual authority are thwarted in the public arena. As God's people we should know that individualism is a dangerous illusion. Christians are to stand against the world, but not alone. Together we are to discern evil in the culture around us, and then work out our response through corporate Bible study, prayer and discussion. And just as important, we are to practice what the Bible teaches about accountability to others in such a way that private professions of faith give powerful public witness.

Individual Christians who get caught in a spirit of privatistic Christianity will face tremendous temptations to divorce faith from obedience, thus laying the axe to the root of Christian effectiveness in society. There are well-known examples of this approach to spirituality. A well-known TV evangelist once commented, "If I said it on the air, I believed it"—as if saying it made it true. This is an illustration of the breakdown between belief and behavior, between "faith" and truth. Just because a person says and believes something does not make it true in the biblical meaning of the word.

I fear that some Christians have not discerned the existential nature of the world around them; nor have they perceived the therapeutic ethos that has developed in our society. Inner spiritual reality is not to be confused with an experiential form of Christianity. Subjective experiences must not be more real than the truths revealed in the Bible.

God's Word and Character

Individual believers and local congregations must be firmly rooted in the fixed realities of God's Word and God's character.

In his booklet *The Devil's Gauntlet* Os Guinness refers to an experience he had while attending one of the leading evangelical churches in Washington, D.C. The call to worship had as its confession on that particular Sunday morning, "Father, forgive us, for we have not lived up to our dreams." Os called this "Hallmark-card theology" and went on to say, "American evangelicalism is awash in a sloppy, sentimental, superficial theology that wouldn't empower a clockwork mouse, let alone a disciple of Christ in the tough modern world."

While there is no argument with those who minister the love of God to a hurting world, the danger of responding to human need without sound, systematic proclamation of biblical truth is very real. To do so will lead to a sentimental kind of Christianity that is more concerned with healing people's emotional wounds than bringing them into right relationship with God. Fortunately, we do not have to choose between these two options.

A crucial moral change has taken place in the Western world. It began with a shift from the Puritan commitment to salvation through self-denial and the cross, and has moved toward a therapeutic value system stressing self-realization through a smorgasbord of self-help and New Age systems. People are often more concerned with physical and psychic health than they are with their true spiritual condition.

Admittedly, people have always been preoccupied with their own emotional and physical well-being. But something different has happened in the past seventy-five years. In the last century, the quest for health and well-being occurred within a larger religious and ethical framework. Now the quest for health is carried out in a world quick to embrace esoteric religious experiences but loath to embrace the death of Christ as their only source of salvation.

Acknowledging one's need of emotional healing, or desiring that from God, is not wrong. But when the larger framework of society is self-realization, and the root problem is not challenged by the preaching of the cross and the need to repent, then believers are in great danger of drifting into a subjective kind of Christianity that has little relationship to sound doctrine.

The Christian's need for emotional healing is no different from the non-Christian's, but if this need is not addressed within the context of God's concern for righteousness in our lives, then we will not become biblical Christians but self-centered egotists who are merely using God to meet personal and private longings.

A culture has emerged in the West that seeks to convince people that to experience reality, sexual happiness and inner well-being, they must *consume.* A close relationship is developing between this consumer culture and the therapeutic ethos of emotional wholeness. Marketing strategists seek systematically to undermine the traditional values of work, savings and the family. Sometimes deliberately and sometimes unwittingly, advertisers and therapists reinforce the spreading culture of consumption and self-realization.

Where does that leave the Church? If the Gospel is peddled as one more way to be happy or rich, then we are products of our culture, rather than beacons within it. When the world cannot tell the difference between the lifestyles of Christians and non-Christians, the Church is in serious trouble. And when prosperity doctrines reflect the cultural ethos of the world more than the biblical faith of our forefathers, the Church must face the reality that she has been shaped by our culture.

What is the answer to this problem? I would suggest two simple requirements: an authoritative, thoughtful proclamation of God's Word; and systematic application of God's character to how we live as Christians. To do this in the cities' present cultural milieu means nothing less than a power encounter with demonic forces.

The purpose for the proclamation of God's Word is more than hearing our favorite denominational doctrine or the pastor's petty theological hobbyhorses. It is to get to know God through His Word. In the process we are to learn about His character: We are to know His justice; we are to understand His mercy; we are to revel in His wisdom; we are to be conformed to His holiness; and we are to stand in awe of His grace.

The Lord spoke this through the prophet Jeremiah many years ago:

> "Let not the wise man glory in his wisdom, let not the mighty man glory in his might, let not the rich man glory in his riches; but let him who glories glory in this, that he

understands and knows me, that I am the Lord who practice steadfast love, justice, and righteousness in the earth; for in these things I delight, says the Lord."

Jeremiah 9:23–24

Such preaching means work, particularly for those called as ministers. A story is told of a young man who went to an experienced pastor and asked for advice on how to prepare his first sermon. The pastor told him, "Son, don't try to fill your mind with the learning of men or with fancy thoughts. Simply pray and ask the Lord to speak to you when you stand in the pulpit. When you do that I guarantee God will speak to you."

So taking the advice of his pastor the young man did not study or prepare ahead of time. In faith he believed that when he stood in the pulpit God would speak to him.

When the momentous Sunday came the young man stood, proud of himself for not allowing his mind to be filled with "human thoughts." He stood quietly and prayed a simple prayer: "Lord, I am your humble servant. I have come now to preach Your Word. Please speak to me."

And the Lord spoke. He said: *My son, you are not prepared.*

This story may be far more true than we care to acknowledge. How many pastors prepare their sermons a few hours before they rush to the pulpit? How many have not taken the time to seek God and study His Word, coming to the pulpit assured of what God wants to say to His people? To quote Os Guinness,

The problem is not just the heresy, though doubtless there is some of that. Nor is it just the degree of entertainment, and there is lots of that. Nor is it even the

appalling gaps in the theology, for there is far too much of that. The real problem is that in what is said there is almost no sense of announcement from God; in what is shown, there is almost no sense of anointing by God.
(*The Devil's Gauntlet*, p. 25)

The Sunday morning pulpit is not a time for preachers to expound their own good ideas. It is a time for them to proclaim the eternal Word of God and to do it with wisdom, understanding, authority and anointing, being particularly careful to discern evil powers and how they are attacking God's people. They are to stand as ministers who know God and teach the people about His character. The written Word is to be made alive by the flame of the Spirit burning in their hearts as they have spent hours alone with God, hearing what He would say to His people and saying it with conviction.

Worship

Worship of the living God is a power encounter of the highest order. Ascribing to any object, or being, the devotion that belongs to God is sin; it is yielding to the temptation the devil presented to Jesus in the wilderness. Satan seeks to lure us if he can, and manipulate us if he cannot, to redirect our worship and trust away from the living God.

Not only does Satan tempt us to worship false gods; he also seeks to stifle our right worship by undermining our faith in God. If our ministry focus is dominated by the problems of the city, and we develop a negative outlook, it will affect our worship of God. While problems are not to be ignored or denied, God and His goodness must be central.

God demonstrated to the people of Israel the significance of worship in spiritual warfare by defeating Judah's enemies through the singing of praise instead of military power (2 Chronicles 20:21–22). John Dawson reminds us of this powerful truth in his book *Taking Our Cities for God*:

> The New Testament Greek word for worship, *proskuneo*, means "to kiss toward," implying emotional response toward God. Our heartfelt expressions of praise are rooted in the discipline of thanksgiving. To be grateful is consciously to acknowledge our debt to another, and this is an activity we are to choose: "Always and for everything giving thanks in the name of our Lord Jesus Christ to God the Father" (Ephesians 5:20).
>
> The opposite behavior—murmuring and complaining —is a sin that God will not tolerate. Such conduct poisons the atmosphere, robs others of their faith and produces death and defeat. When the children of Israel murmured against Moses and Aaron, 14,700 of them were smitten with a plague and died (see Numbers 16:49).

Dawson goes on to point out that while we hesitate to slander people openly and directly, we think it is acceptable to murmur against our cities because of their supposedly impersonal nature. The issue that motivated Israel's complaint against Moses was also their environment: "Moreover you have not brought us into a land flowing with milk and honey, nor given us inheritance of fields and vineyards" (Numbers 16:14).

I have heard countless Christians slander the city as if the reality of the problems excused their negative attitudes. Such criticalness is a breeding ground for unbelief. They focus on the problems and become more impressed with Satan's power than God's. Sin in a city *is* offensive to the spiritually sensitive person. It is grievous to see pollution hovering in gray clouds over large cities. It is hurtful to one's spirit to see large numbers of young men and women being exploited by sex-mad pimps and purveyors of pornography. Anger seems the only appropriate response to the oppression and injustice highlighted in third-world urban slum areas and first-world inner cities. Dirt and destruction in cities are offensive.

But the key issue is how we should respond to all this. It exists. It is evil. It is repugnant to see. But should we respond with hardness of heart and criticalness?

What has this to do with worship in the city? Worship is more than what we do for an hour or two on Sundays. It is an attitude of life. It is a lifestyle. It is being focused on the goodness of God and the assurance of His desire to bless all people in spite of the corruption and arrogance of sinful humanity.

Without worship we will be overwhelmed by the needs of the city. We will develop cynicism and unbelief. Our service to God will be tainted by bitterness. Our existence will be motivated by escape. We will be dominated by the city instead of rising above its problems.

Worship creates a highway from God's heart to ours. We see the city, in spite of its problems, in the light of God's destiny for His people in that place. We begin to see with eyes of faith what God wants to do in and through His people.

Regular corporate worship magnifies what is in the hearts of individuals as well. If we come with a heart of thanksgiving that is fueled by regular study of God's Word and focus on His character, worship with the community of believers feeds our souls.

The presence of worshiping Christians in a needy city is a powerful challenge to the powers of darkness. We are threatening the hold of Satan on people's lives—a hold strengthened by the illusion that he is all-powerful.

Research and Analysis

Another spiritual weapon for contesting Satan's efforts to destroy the city is to research the issues that weaken the influence of the Gospel in the city. There is a deep-rooted anti-intellectualism in the Church that has caused us to be ineffective not only in reaching thinking non-Christians, but in influencing the direction of our culture. When we do not encourage use of the intellectual gifts that God has given the Church, we are being disobedient, anti-spiritual and unloving. Only through a tough-minded analysis of the political, economic and social issues that face us in the city can we hope to exercise the influence that God has intended us to have. This is a matter of Christian faithfulness and integrity.

Sanctified minds need to examine the influence of culture *in its totality* on the Church. Every part of life is impregnated by a culture totally at odds with godliness and Christian witness. Spiritual warfare at this point pulls down strongholds by hard thinking. We need prayer, yes, but we also need prophetic sociologists to point out the betrayal of the Gospel in our culture.

Worldliness attacks the Church by luring us into compromise on the absolutes of our faith. But we are also tempted to participate in unethical fund-raising, superficial fellowship, ungodly dependence on technology, manipulation by information systems and compromise with the world's educational philosophies and techniques. Unless we are thinking carefully about our lifestyles and how they affect our financial dealings, our relationships, the use of our time, our ambitions and dreams and our families, we will soon be swallowed up into a society that pulls us away from biblical Christianity in the most basic functions of life. If Christians are not aware how totally dependent they have become on the world's systems, we will be overwhelmed by one of Satan's most subtle but devastating attacks on the Church in the last 2,000 years.

We must not soothe our consciences by giving handouts to the poor and counseling the wounded. Nor can we look at any increasing numbers in our churches and feel smug. If we develop a narrow agenda of social and moral issues and pat ourselves on the back as if we have done enough, we delude ourselves.

We must repent for turning the great ideals of liberty and prosperity into modern-day idols. Liberty and prosperity are adored as the goals of life, rather than appreciated as the result of honesty and hard work. We have been blinded by these idols so that we cannot see the multitude of evils that are taking place in the economic and social arenas around us.

Fervent Intercession

If we are to discern the battlefronts rightly, not only must we think in a tough-minded manner, but we must be linked with fervent intercessors who are listening carefully to what God has on His heart for our cities. A group of women associated with Christ Our Shepherd Church in Washington,

D.C., were praying for that city in 1984. During the time of prayer, one of the women felt that the Lord was putting it on her heart to intercede for the influence astrology had on Nancy Reagan. At that time it had not been made public that Mrs. Reagan was seeking the counsel of an astrologer. When the news broke several years later, the prayer group felt it was in response to their prayers that God would expose what was "hidden in darkness."

Intercession is not an occupation for little old ladies who have nothing better to do with their time; it stands central to the Church's mission in society. Windows of insight are given through intercession that should be linked to those fighting on the intellectual front. Nehemiah joined those working on the walls of Jerusalem, telling them that if the enemy attacked in one place they should blow their trumpets to rally the help of others. This integration of intercession and intellectual pursuit of truth is vital. If they stand alone they may produce either a warmhearted but ill-informed zeal on the one hand, or a coldhearted and aloof intellectualism on the other.

Those who take seriously the call to intercede for the city must guard against a detachment that keeps them from identifying with the people they are praying for. Identification with people makes our praying real.

I have the privilege not only of living in a major inner city, but of traveling constantly, speaking about our work. I love the thrill of declaring God's purposes for cities to audiences large and small. But being away from direct ministry on the streets due to my speaking schedule and being saddled with inescapable administrative responsibilities has taken its toll. I sometimes find myself speaking about experiences from further and further in the past, without up-to-date contact with people in my neighborhood. Sometimes I am forced to accept this as part of the price of an international calling to challenge others to get involved.

I must be vigilant, however, to notice any coldheartedness due to lack of identification and intercession. When my prayer life suffers from lack of discipline, everything else is affected. Sermon illustrations become just that: sermon illustrations.

But when I pray with passion, and when I identify with the sins of the people (Nehemiah 1), things begin to change. Not only do I speak with a greater authority, but my life back in Amsterdam is touched more deeply. I get more involved with people spontaneously, and I partake in the spiritual heart-throb of the city. Prayer keeps me from being a spectator. Identification keeps me in tune on a heart level.

When we prepare a team to go to another city from Amsterdam for evangelism, we first do research into the historical, cultural and spiritual background of the city. When the team arrives they walk the streets two-by-two, interceding until they sense that they have discerned the spiritual forces that are at work. They then pray specifically for breakthroughs in these areas. This kind of intercession is not a substitute for residency or analysis of issues, but is central to all forms of spiritual warfare. It provides the link to God's heart, and the integration point for the total mission effort. It is the "nervous system" of the Church's response to evil powers, linking all our efforts in a concerted and coordinated response.

Prayer teams are desperately needed by those who are engaged in the public arena, and vice-versa. Satan uses people to obstruct the purposes of God—even well-meaning believers. Many a sincere politician or public servant has found his greatest opposition coming from other Christians. This should not surprise us. It was Peter who told Jesus He should not go to Jerusalem to die on the cross. Recognizing the source of Peter's grand idea, Jesus looked at Peter and spoke to Satan: "Get behind me, Satan!" It is through prayer—the exercising of the authority we have in Jesus' name—that we win spiritual battles.

We see this marriage of mind and spirit, prayer and research, in the life of Nehemiah. Nehemiah heard a report about the broken walls of Jerusalem while he was in exile in Babylon. He was so disturbed by the report that it moved him to days of fasting, prayer and weeping over the spiritual state of his people. When he finally received permission to return to Jerusalem to do something about this problem, before he announced any plans or launched any programs, he surveyed the walls of the city very carefully. Nehemiah took time to examine the walls to make sure he understood their exact condition. What he saw when he looked them over confirmed what he had discerned through prayer.

There is a great need in Christian leadership for those who are both brokenhearted and tough-minded, people who are dove-gentle and yet serpent-wise. This kind of Christianity can be a great tool in the hands of God and a great weapon against the forces of darkness.

Church Unity

The unity of the Church in the city aids warfare against spiritual powers. The apostle Paul declares that we are seated with Christ in the **heavenly places**, *together* with all the saints:

> Even when we were dead through our trespasses, [God] made us alive together with Christ (by grace you have been saved), and raised us up with him, and made us sit with him in the heavenly places in Christ Jesus.
>
> Ephesians 2:5–6

This implies that authority as a united Church comes from being seated with Christ in His place of divine rule. Notice how often Paul writes *us* and *our* in this passage.

The context is our victory over evil and the powers of darkness (Ephesians 2:2). Paul paints a picture for us of a Church that is seated *together* with Christ in His place of authority ruling over the powers; but he makes it clear that our authority is related directly to our unity.

Lived out, this truth points the way to openness, interdependence and accountability as a way of life. Most believers are shocked, however, at the thought of seeking advice about their family and business dealings, much less other personal decisions. Has the Church lost her spiritual authority because we compromise this vital element of biblical Church life? The influence of modernism may be so pervasive that we find that many natural and spontaneous actions in the early Church are extraneous to our way of thinking.

It seems from a casual reading of Scripture that the elders of New Testament churches were functioning in close relationship with one another. This "connectedness" of church leaders is missing today, and I believe the Church will not have the authority promised in Scripture until it is restored. The unity implied in Ephesians 2 is dynamic and powerful. It is achieved not passively but by active pursuit.

We must realize that any differences in perspective or emphasis among Christians today are minor compared to the battles being fought by the whole Church against the powers in the city. We must rise above our normal theological differences, allow one another freedom to be wrong sometimes and find common ground to stand together in Christ. We must do this because we know that "God opposes the proud, but gives grace to the humble" (James 4:6).

Where biblical unity exists, we can disagree lovingly and still get on with the business of setting people free from sin and challenging the powers and their influence on public institutions and policy. This unity will express itself in a spirit of teachableness and servanthood. By maintaining a humble and teachable attitude, while holding to our personal theological convictions, we can fellowship with believers of various denominations. This paves the way to build the kind of unity in a city that is absolutely essential for overcoming spiritual powers.

The Moravians used to teach that fellowship among Christians was a sacrament of the Church, a way God gave grace to His people. City life has become so hectic, so filled with sensory overload, that it leaves people emotionally depleted. The temptation is to narrow our contacts with other believers to the point that is necessary for "survival." When this happens we may have more time for ourselves, but we are on dangerous ground spiritually.

If we are cut off from meaningful relationships with other believers, Satan wins a victory and the first step has been taken to denigrate the Church. City believers need fellowship with other Christians, and they will have to fight the busyness of the city to do so. We cannot afford to be without the teaching, prayer, worship and intercession that we were created for.

If the Church in the city is going to be radically Christian, it will be a Church that seeks at all costs to build unity within the whole Body of Christ. Are our programs so sacrosanct, or are we so busy that we dare not . . .

- Invite ministers from other churches in the city to speak from our pulpits?
- Set aside time regularly to visit other congregations and Christian organizations to see what they are doing?
- Set up sister-church relationships so that every white suburban church is in direct relationship with a black, Asian, Hispanic, Chinese, Cambodian, Vietnamese or African congregation somewhere in the city?
- Have families from other ethnic backgrounds in our homes for meals, and vice-versa?
- Close down the Sunday services once a quarter so that our congregation can visit other congregations?
- Build joint Sunday school and youth programs with other churches?
- Adopt a small church and provide financial and human resources to enable that church to get established?
- Make appointments with one or more members of another church and go for regular prayer walks with them through the city?
- Conduct joint missions conferences with several other churches so that we can share in one another's strengths and blessings together?
- Bring boards of deacons or elders from different churches

together for fellowship in order to break down fears and mistrust?

• Pray for other churches in the city on Sunday mornings from the pulpit, particularly those churches that we do not like or agree with theologically?

• Conduct joint evangelistic outreaches at Christmas and Easter?

Most likely you do not have time to participate in all these activities. But every Christian must take time for the genuine fellowship that is characterized by accountability and honesty with other believers if he is to be a biblical Christian. It really boils down to a matter of obedience. If we are going to think and act like Christians, then we must be willing to cut back on work and pleasure activities, demote the television and lead our families into meaningful friendship with other believers and our church community. As we make that commitment we will experience the authority promised us in Ephesians 2:6.

Does this kind of unity make a difference in the city? I know it does. In 1973 I arrived in Amsterdam after a long trip through central Asia and Eastern Europe from Afghanistan. When I arrived in Amsterdam the thought came to me that I should pray for many other organizations, denominations and Christians to come to the city. This conviction grew as I began to visit local pastors and research the history of the Church in Amsterdam. I could find only a handful of evangelical con-gregations, and it was obvious that Christians in the city were defeated, divided and discouraged.

Those partnering with me began to pray actively that God would bring church planters, pastors, prophets, evangelists, Christian workers, laymen and preachers out of retirement to the city. We focused our prayer on traditional churches and we prayed for new churches.

God answered our prayers richly. We have seen many pastors come out of retirement to accept the call of various denominations. New churches have been planted in neighborhoods around the city—not because church members have changed congregations, but because the unsaved are coming to know Jesus Christ. Many Christian organizations have come to the city. We feel at one in heart and purpose with these pastors and organizations because we have prayed for them so much.

Some do not know the amount of time and prayer we have given to them. There was a period of several years when we prayed every noon hour for pastors and leaders by name. We would call ministers in the city and ask them what their prayer needs were. Some were shocked. Many of them were theologically liberal or even unsaved. It made no difference to us. We were committed to praying for them.

The prayer paid off. Though we still have our problems, there is a healthy spirit of respect and love in the city of Amsterdam among Christian leaders. We have had joint celebrations. We have gone on prayer walks together. We have sent workers to one another and supported one another with finances and other resources. This kind of unity is possible and it does make a difference in the spiritual climate of the city.

Residence in the City

This last category of spiritual weapons has to do with residence in the city. Whether in a suburb or a ghetto, whether a neighborhood populated by people from Asia or Mexico or the West Indies, whether in high-rise apartments or tenement houses, God is calling Christians to lay down their aspirations and dreams of comfort and security, and commit themselves to God-directed residency within the city.

This is a biblical principle. Jesus is our example. He gave up His home. He gave up the comfort of heaven. He gave up the closeness of being with His Father. He gave up wealth and honor. He laid aside His divine rights in order to live among us.

If we are going to follow the example of the Lord Jesus, as we are commanded to do in Scripture, then the basis of where we choose to live will not be what kind of equity it will bring in a house, or what kind of physical safety we judge it will provide us, but whether it is where God wants us. Spiritual warfare in this context means committing ourselves to a neighborhood of people to demonstrate the Gospel to them in word and deed. That means residency.

I challenge you to pray about moving out of your neighborhood, and moving into one with less economic status or one populated by an ethnic minority group in order to learn from them and give to them of what God has put into your life. If you stay where you are, let it be because of calling, not comfort. (For a fuller discussion of this principle of residency, see chapter 6.)

Servant residency means more than owning a house and driving back and forth to work. It means involvement in the institutions and structures of your neighborhood. It means putting our children into local schools and getting involved with parent-teacher organizations. It means listening to the expressed needs of our neighbors and reflecting them in the way we campaign and vote in local city elections. It means visiting city hall and letting our voices be heard. True residency means that we follow the admonition of Jeremiah, writing to the exiles of Israel in the city of Babylon: "Seek the welfare of the city where I have sent you into exile, and pray to the Lord on its behalf, for in its welfare you will find your welfare" (Jeremiah 29:7).

By repenting of overconsumption, rejecting fear and concern for our own well-being and responding to the challenge of servant residence, we are engaging ourselves in battle against spiritual powers in the city that are determined to divide races and isolate Christians. Many neighborhoods are constructed to protect the very cultural values that separate us. By refusing to adopt the limits of a security-conscious society, we are taking steps toward meaningful witness as Christians. This is not to say we cannot be witnesses to Christ if we live in "nice" neighborhoods and it is not to say we should be reckless about our safety, but it does say we are willing to challenge spiritual strongholds that have kept many from Christ by overcoming personal fears and prejudices, turning aside from opportunities of financial gain and living primarily to serve others.

By choosing to live in a run-down suburb or slum area, we are practicing Christ's command to overcome evil with good. By responding in the opposite spirit to crime, violence, greed and fear, we are taking steps to conquer the powers. Yes, there is risk. Our children will be hassled at school, our homes will be broken into and our well-patterned lives will be disturbed. But if we do not step out of the comfort zones we build around ourselves, can we say we have truly taken up our crosses to follow Jesus?

There are fears to overcome, but God does not call us to a work He will not uphold. In the next two chapters, we will be looking at the city from God's perspective, and allowing that to challenge our beliefs and some of our more serious misconceptions.

Part 2
The Meaning of the City

4
Looking for a
City Built by God

God planned cities. We can know with certainty that He wanted us to gather in city-communities because He created us for togetherness. The Lord made this clear in the opening pages of the Bible when He commanded Adam and Eve to multiply and fill the earth (Genesis 1:27–28).

The longing for "togetherness" is tapped when we experience meaningful fellowship with other believers. But that is to be a starting point, not the sum total of its meaning. We are to go on from there to be God's people in the place where we live, providing a taste of true love and joy by touching other people's lives around us.

Knowing this, we have a biblical frame of reference for understanding cities. They are among the places God intends us to live together, expressing our various cultures and living out our commitments to fulfill His plan for our lives: "He made from one every nation of men to live on all the face of the earth" (Acts 17:26).

It is amazing how much we believe in the sovereignty of God but how much we resist the idea that the city is God's creation. God can do anything, it seems, as long as we approve! Not only did God intend for Adam and Eve to plant a city in a garden, He has continued to call cities into being. The Bible states clearly that God draws up the "boundaries of man's habitation" (Acts 17:26). He is actively fulfilling His original plan to bring people together to fulfill His purposes. And that means cities—large and small.

Does this mean everyone must live in a city? The question misses the point. The size of a city should not be the determining factor in our decisions about where to live, nor should the social climate or value of property sway us. Where does God want me? Where will my life count most for Him? How best can I serve Him in a place? What is on His heart for a community? These are the questions Kingdom people should be asking.

Large cities are nothing more than a collection of various communities, networks of people, if you wish, brought together in one place. Realistically, we cannot serve more than one of the networks or communities of people in a given city. So the focus for finding God's will should not be the "largeness" of a place, but the "rightness" of God's call to those whom we are called to serve and live among.

While a small town may be said to have a single culture, large cities contain many cultures. We must learn to think in terms of peoplehood, not place; of serving, not circumstances. Most Western Christians are very ethnocentric. They stick to their own kind, blind to the new reality: God is shaking up the world. The city is being used by God to bring peoples to each other and to Himself.

When God created the city, His plans were—and are—good; it is man who fell, not God. And it is still God's love that brings people together. God could sovereignly stop the worldwide urbanization taking place, but He has not done so. He is, in fact, urging on the process. I urge you not to view the rapid urbanization of our planet and your nation as a "sign of the times" but to see it as the work of a loving Father seeking to bring His creation together that we might rediscover His purpose for our lives.

If people refuse to submit to God, then in His love for them He will use the close proximity of other selfish people to reveal their need for Him. Nothing can deter Him from using the city to accomplish His will.

Christians are the ones who seem to be most resistant to God's urbanizing the world. Perhaps the spirit of worldliness has entered the hearts of believers more than we realize. When the first criterion for making decisions is "Will it make me happy, secure and comfortable?" something has gone desperately wrong in the Church. Do we believe that God would dare ask us to sacrifice what we want in order to serve Him?

The purpose of developing an urban theology is not just to respond to the pessimism and anti-urban prejudice found among most Christians, but to help us respond obediently to God.

The Bible is an eschatological book, recording God's purposes for all of human history. The making and remaking of this world begins and ends within the first and last pages of the Bible. Between its covers, the Bible unfolds God's redemptive plan for the whole creation.

The fact that history ends in a city, the New Jerusalem, gives us greater clarity about how it was intended to begin. The picture of the people of God gathered around the throne in the New Jerusalem fulfills God's original purposes for Adam and Eve. The marriage feast of the Lamb in the heavenly city speaks of the celebration that God wants when His creation gathers together, not only for eternity, but right now.

Having begun this planet with those purposes, God has not changed His mind. Through urbanization, the redemptive heart of God is at work drawing His creation back to Himself. If we do not love cities we are missing out on His redemptive work on this planet.

A Biblical Definition of the City

What is a city?

The city is first of all *people*, created by God and gathered together to serve Him and live for His glory. It is also the *place* where His people are called to be stewards over the resources and environment of His creation, living in peace with one another and submitting to just magistrates who govern according to God's laws.

There are several vital elements in such a definition. The first is people. A "gathered people" is a community, with all the responsibilities any civilized, much less Christian, community has toward God and one another. Like Abraham of old, we long for a city "whose builder and maker is God" (Hebrews 11:10). This longing for togetherness is planted deep within us by God. It is our destiny to be together for eternity, and that longing manifests itself in the here and now by our wanting love, friendship, marriage, companionship and Christian fellowship.

The second element of our definition is place. We will discuss this in greater detail later (chapter 6), so it will suffice to say here that God chooses places for His people to gather. This means incarnation. It means we invest ourselves, create residency, put down our roots, with the intention to give to the place God has called us.

Still another important dimension of our definition of the city is stewardship. God gave Adam and Eve dominion over the earth, not to use it up as quickly as possible (which our economies of growth seem to imply), but to rule over it wisely so that it is used in a godly fashion. Surely the problem of urban pollution and smog (of which suburban commuters are major contributors—we must remember that the next time we abhor the "dirty inner city") is a reminder that we have failed miserably in this regard.

Another dimension of the definition of the city is harmonious relationships. When we are told by well-meaning people that Christians should stay out of politics because the Church should deal solely with spiritual matters, we face a dilemma. It is God's will that races live in harmony with one another, and that the rich should not exploit the poor. When these sins exist in society, the Church must speak up. We cannot be silent because someone feels that "getting involved in politics" is none of our business. We must not be silent in the face of sin, whether it be the sins of an individual or an entire city. God is a God of justice. The city is God's idea. Everything that happens in the city, therefore, is of vital importance to the concerned Christian.

Lastly, a city is to have God-fearing magistrates who govern righteously. When that happens it bodes well for the citizens of the city. But when there is corruption, injustice, power-seeking and political maneuvering, the city will not fulfill its God-given purpose.

The Sacred Place

There is much evidence of urban theology in the Bible. A clear urban tradition is found throughout the Scriptures that is both positive in nature and points to God's esteem for the places where He calls His people. This tradition of the "sacred place," as Ray Bakke calls it (*The Urban Christian*), assures us that where God's people are, He is in their midst.

In the Old Testament, the people often built altars to remember the great things God did for them in a particular place. Sometimes it was answered prayer; at other times it was victory in battle or unique spiritual experiences. God's people were not afraid to look upon those special places as sacred. Jacob regarded the place of his dream in the desert as holy. He called it *Bethel*—Hebrew for "house of God."

We can look upon any place as holy, including the most ungodly office environment or poorest neighborhood. They are equally important to the Lord. This means New York City is as sacred to the Lord as Calcutta or Liverpool or Belfast. If we abhor any city it is more a reflection on us than on the city.

Cities As Personalities

God's concern is not only for individuals, but also for groups of people. He calls and makes covenants with families, tribes and nations. His covenants with Noah, Abraham and David and their descendants testify to the unique love God has for the "peoples" He has brought into being.

It is typical of people from post-industrial Western cultures to look at the rest of the world through individualistic eyes, rather than seeing extended families and peoples. This is reflected in the lack of distinction between the singular and plural *you* in our modern English language. The result is an uphill battle to perceive our calling to covenant "peoplehood." We interpret promises in the Bible that were given to the Body of Christ and the nation of Israel very privately.

Because of this, we miss the significance of those portions of Scripture that speak to cities as personalities. Judgment is often pronounced on whole cities, and not on particular individuals in them. Cities are often described as having personal (female) characteristics. In Ezekiel 16 Jerusalem is condemned for "her" sins and the prophet goes on to refer to her "sisters" Sodom and Samaria.

Blessings are also pronounced on entire cities. In Jeremiah 29:7, as we have seen, the exiles in Babylon are told to "seek the welfare of the city." It was not particular individuals they were told to bless, but the city as a whole. God saw the city collectively, addressing her need for being cared for in this amazing passage of collective grace.

This commitment to the whole city is dynamic in the book of Isaiah. In Isaiah 61 the prophet refers to the Lord's plans for the renewed city, a dream that is to be consummated in the New Jerusalem. This is the city that Jesus weeps for many years later, and speaks to when He prophesies to her of her collective spiritual blindness (Luke 19:41–43). In Isaiah 60 the Lord promises that her walls will be built up and kings will minister to her.

A city takes on a spiritual life of her own. The city is more than the sum of her individuals. The prophecies concerning Damascus, Philistia, Tyre, Edom and Moab in the book of Amos are warnings to us that we cannot turn a blind eye to the spiritual state of the city in which we live. We cannot escape our responsibility by moving to another part of the city, or leaving it altogether.

The spiritual and historical backgrounds of a city are interrelated. Just as the actions of her past influence the street prostitute to take up her trade, so the past actions of people in the city influence the city's spiritual development. And just as a raped woman struggles for acceptance, a city plundered by unrighteous merchants will bear the marks of the injustice in her corporate psyche.

Who Is Responsible for the City?

Over and over again cities are referred to in the Bible as corporate entities, with personalities and spiritual characters that the people of God in that city are held responsible for (Ezekiel 27; Zephaniah 2:15; Revelation 2–3; 18:7).

It is not the architecture that gives a city her personality and spiritual state, but the collective decisions of her people. It was not the presence of unrighteous people that finally brought destruction on Sodom, but the absence of ten righteous men. And it was the sins of robbery, injustice and violence that brought the judgment of the Lord against Samaria (Amos 3). The decisions of merchant organizations and city councils, as well as the collective morality of the people, are what turn a loose-knit group of people into a legal and spiritual body.

God Has Plans for the City

It is also true that if cities have collective personalities, it is possible for them to do justice collectively. The central role that Jerusalem played in the spiritual history of Israel speaks to the plans that God sets in motion for whole cities. This is confirmed when we study the role of the cities of refuge in the Old Testament. God wanted to use these cities—that is, the collective citizenry and their appointed magistrates—to serve those who needed protection in society.

God intended that the cities of the land of Canaan be a blessing and not a curse. Deuteronomy 6:10 speaks of "great and goodly cities." Cities served different purposes for the children of Israel, including storehouse cities, cities of defense and spiritual centers of renewal and blessing (Numbers 35:1–34; 2 Chronicles 8:5–6; 11:5; Deuteronomy 16:18; Psalm 72:16; and Proverbs 11).

She Is Fallen

Sadly, sin has spoiled God's plan for cities. Cain built the first city after Adam and Eve aborted God's purposes in the Garden, and called it Enoch, meaning "my beginning." The tendency to independence and pride in cities is self-evident. But this has not always been the case. Some evangelists have experienced responses from entire cities to the preaching of the Gospel. Charles Finney, George Whitefield and the Welshman Evan Roberts saw great moves of God in cities. What Jonah experienced in Nineveh was certainly no small thing.

Throughout the Old Testament, kings established their

power by building cities to glorify themselves and their em-
pires. This fed into Satan's scheme to corrupt God's urban
plans. "Kill the sons of the king of Babylon," cries the prophet
Isaiah, "lest they cover the earth with their cities" (see Isaiah
14:21).

Modern cities tend to be more pluralistic and culturally
diverse. It is as if there are many villages from different nations and cultures piled on top of each other. This complicates
both the spiritual nature of cities and the process of bringing
them the Gospel. One of the most tragic mistakes the Church
can make is to fail to discern the complex and diverse spiritual
personality of modern cities.

Strategies for citywide mass evangelism must be decentral-
ized if they are to be effective. We must take the Gospel to
peoples rather than expect them to come to us. We must learn
the languages of the peoples of the city, and move in culturally sensitive methods. Incarnation and proclamation must
never be separated in the city—or the consequences are tragic.

Pieter Bos, architect and city planner, and now a missionary
in Amsterdam, writes in *City Cries*:

> In modern cities decisions are often made haphazardly
> and with no regard for God. As a result, the city falls
> under the influence of the principalities and powers of
> Satan. Satan uses the anonymous nature of the city as an
> environment which encourages the growth of evil. Peo-
> ple flock to the cities seduced by the lie that there they
> will survive. The results are evident in the environment,
> in the economy, in social problems and in resistance to
> the gospel.   (p. 4)

Though intended by God to serve His purposes, cities are
fallen. Most Christians believe that cities are a necessary evil.

Tolerate them if you must and avoid them if you can. Most of us believe God created man, and man created the city. Following this logic, the very existence of cities is a fruit of the Fall, a result of man's rebellion against God and, therefore, inherently evil. According to this view, Satan is the rightful ruler over the cities, not God. But this is not substantiated by Scriptures. This view is more laden with sociological pessimism than biblical insight.

Cities are no more intrinsically evil than mankind is. Though man is sinful by nature, he is created in the image of God. The same is true for cities. Though their present form is marred by personal and corporate sin, it is God who created mankind for community, and community for mankind.

Just as we are called to love fallen men and women with the love of God, we should love and respect the city. We should see the city for what she was intended to be, and not just for what we think she has become. I say "what we think she has become" because all too often our fear of urban life is far worse than reality. There is a tendency, moreover, to develop an evangelical subculture that baptizes certain values and lifestyles and calls them holy, when they are nothing more than expressions of our own selfishness, fear and cultural myopia.

Redeeming the City

So far I have said that the city is God's idea, that He intends the city to be a blessing and not a curse, that cities have collective personalities and spiritual characters of their own, that the evil character of a city develops because of the individual and corporate choices men make and that believers are responsible for the spiritual well-being of their cities.

When we compare what the Bible says about God's purpose for cities, and what is happening in many cities today, we become more convinced than ever of two things: A tremendous spiritual battle is being fought for control of the city, and many Christians have abandoned the battle. Not all Christians, I must point out. For many believers, the city is home. I know many Asian, black and Hispanic believers who have embraced the city and celebrate its life daily.

What is the implication of these truths for Christians? Though there are many, three stand out with particular importance and urgency. First, we must repent of our urban prejudices and cultivate God's love in our hearts for the city. This will not come without prayer and repentance for any lack of love. And love will not grow without personal involvement with people in the city. It will not grow without relationship. Are you prepared to get involved in genuine friendship with people in the city? Have them in your home? Visit theirs?

Second, through intercession and listening to God, through research and study and through listening to God's people who are already in the city, we must discern God's unique role for the city we live in. By studying its spiritual history and by looking carefully at what God's people are presently doing, we can gain a sense of perspective and appreciation for the continuity of God's work in the place to which He has called us. We are not stepping into a spiritual vacuum. God has been at work, and by discerning what He has been doing through the years, we can develop greater understanding of what is on His heart.

And last, Christians and church leaders must provide servant leadership to the city. By loving the city, being involved in its daily affairs, calling it into account for its unrighteousness, proclaiming the Gospel, participating in its institutions and affirming its strengths, Christians begin to fulfill Christ's mandate to be in the world but not of the world.

We Christians do not take ourselves seriously enough. Our role is to be more than spectator prophets, coming out of our spiritual closets on occasion to march against pornography, only to disappear until we get sufficiently riled up over another issue. We have an ongoing and significant role that can be fulfilled or failed, but never denied. We are God's covenant people, gathered by Him to serve the city, to be stewards over its resources, to bring peace, to prophesy and to lead it in righteousness and justice.

5
Urban Myths and Biblical Realities

Myth *A notion based more on tradition or convenience than on fact.*

Urban myth *A belief that* **1.** *Nature is closer to God than industrialization;* **2.** *The city is impersonal;* **3.** *Cities are totally crime-ridden and dangerous;* **4.** *The city is not a safe place to raise children;* **5.** *The city cannot be changed.*

This century has been characterized as the century of revolution, war and information; perhaps we will even be called the century of achievement if we do not destroy ourselves first. But nothing we have done as the human race has affected our lives so universally as the decision to flock together in cities in such great numbers.

There are several reasons on a human level why so many people have migrated to cities: employment, education, escape from famine and starvation and, if we are more fortunate than most, to enjoy wealth and achievements. That people have flocked to the city with such speed and in such great numbers is what is so remarkable.

The Century of the City

While Christians have been moving out of cities, plenty of others have been moving in. In 1980 there were about 175 cities in the world each with a population exceeding one million. In 1989 there were 348. By the end of the century that number will swell to almost 500. By the year 2000, the sixty largest cities of the world will hold 650 million people.

More than 450 million people have moved to cities since 1945, and according to United Nations estimates, another 500 million will flood cities throughout this last decade of the century. Humankind is changing with breathtaking speed into an urban species. U.N. demographers characterize the movement as "the greatest mass migration in human history."

It is estimated that in 1900 one in twenty people worldwide lived in a city. Today, one in two people live in cities, and by the year 2020, three out of four people will be urban inhabitants.

These numbers help us grasp the reality of the urbanization of the planet, but very few of us have stopped to think through the implications that such rapid social change means for our lives personally.

In the preceding chapter, I tried to lay a biblical foundation for looking at the city through God's eyes. To go further, it is necessary to examine the prejudices we have against the city. Prejudice is always rooted in a stereotype, which results in not only fear and rejection, but believing a lie. Believing a lie, or a myth, justifies our actions, at least to ourselves.

Are there truths in our stereotypes? Most definitely, but they are often half-truths and generalizations shaped by one or two limited experiences or an unforgiven incident. Many of our prejudices are inherited from our parents and friends, and then reinforced by our own limited contact with the people we mistrust.

The truth about ourselves and our myths will be found by examining carefully all sides of a thing, then drawing objective conclusions. More importantly, truth is found by seeing people and situations from God's perspective. What looks good and acceptable to a callous sinner takes on a different perspective when that person is broken by God's love.

To see the city as God sees it is not merely an intellectual exercise. And to explode the myths that have justified our reticence to embrace the city with God's love will require more than reading a book or hearing a sermon. There must be ruthless pursuit of truth on our knees. The ground of our heart must be broken up so that we can be in the right state to receive spiritual insight from the Lord.

I am compelled to ask if you are truly committed to such an exercise.

Pulling Down Idols in Our Minds

A myth can quickly become an idol, a spiritual hiding place. It can become holy to us, something we will not and cannot let go. Like the myths of old, our personal myths can become objects of veneration. They become like gods to us. They occupy a place of such importance that they are more important than God Himself. A myth about the city becomes an idol in our hearts when it prevents us from loving the city with God's love and being anxious to do whatever the Lord wants us to do to serve the city.

When we cannot hear and obey God's voice to love the city and live in it because of enslavement to false values and ungodly fears, we have become slaves to our idols. It is in that state that myths take root in our hearts. We believe them in order to justify our disobedience.

The call to see the city with the eyes of God runs contrary to the doctrine that God wants all Christians to be financially successful and materially prosperous. These doctrines undermine sacrifice and make it very difficult for Christians to lay down their lives for the sake of others.

We will examine some of our Christian myths in this chapter. I will try to do so in an objective manner; there are elements of truth in our urban myths. We want to acknowledge the very real problems of our great cities, and find the biblical realities.

One needs only to examine the consequences of our urban myths to realize their harmfulness: fear, despair, abandonment, paralysis of action, separation of believers and millions of people suffering without practical or spiritual help. Let's look at some of the more prevalent myths that have been used to justify the Church's retreat from the city.

Myth Number One: Nature Is Closer to God than the City

Harvie Conn points out that in one survey it was found that 91.4% of all evangelical Christians in the United States live outside large cities of one million or more (*A Clarified Vision for Urban Mission*, p. 17). The vision of the Church in that nation and her role in society is being shaped by rural and suburban theologians. It is no wonder that it is so difficult to recruit urban missionaries from America or to stimulate evangelical involvement in the inner cities.

This has not always been the case. During the Middle Ages, Western cities were associated with freedom and self-determination. During the Enlightenment, cities became centers of culture and learning. William Funk points out that the formation of the English language reflects this flattering but passing view of the city. This quote from his book *Word Origins* was printed in Conn, p. 19:

> We city dwellers, at least in ancient days, were supposed to be more civil in our manners and more civilized in our ways than others, for both of these words, *civil* and *civilized*, are the eventual children of the Latin term *civis* which meant "one who lives in the city." All city folks, you see, were regarded as automatically cultured and housebroken. And from the ancient Latin we have borrowed the word *urbs* which also meant city, and we used it to create the word *urbane* which describes the smooth manners that were presumed to be characteristic of metropolitan society. . . . And from the Greek *polis*, "city," we inherited our word *politic*. If you are politic, you are expedient, shrewd, discreet, and artful in your address and your procedure. . . .

Then eighteenth-century industrialization led to urban growth, and poverty and labor exploitation became rampant. People began to fear the city, and came to look upon it as the cause of the problems.

The city became a symbol in people's minds of social disorder and sin. That picture has grown to great proportions. News reports are broadcast nightly into our homes, confirming our worst fears. The news is bad news and it is all about the city.

It is only one step further to build a theology of escape: What we see happening in the city is evil; therefore, the city is evil. The Bible says we should avoid all appearance of evil, so we run from the city. But what we think we see is not always the truth. Cities are like people, and complex problems cannot be dealt with by superficial generalizations.

Some theologians believe that the children of Israel were nomads, and only after the time of Solomon did they as a people attempt to build the first city. The implication is clear: When Solomon lost his wisdom through sexual corruption, the same spirit was spread throughout the land. The people of God lusted after the pleasures of the flesh, as their king had. And it was this lust that led to the Israelites' first cities.

Such a theological construction is appealing to some. The only problem is that it does not fit the biblical realities. In fact, as Conn points out, when the children of Israel were entering the Promised Land, God "encouraged them to see the cities they would now occupy as gifts from Him" (Deuteronomy 6:10–12).

In the United States this myth is linked to the American Dream. That dream is built on a vision of God's blessing, which is manifested in material abundance. Americans know God has blessed them because "we are the richest nation on the face of the earth." But the problems of the city threaten that dream, and they are inconsistent with the doctrine of prosperity.

It is this vision of materialistic Christianity that has alienated the working classes of the world. This kind of superficiality is despised by the revolutionaries of South America who have become embittered because of the injustices of the wealthy toward the poor. Sadly, it is inconceivable to most Americans that many people do not admire their materialism.

I heard one African brother challenge the concept that materialism and wealth are a valid measure of God's blessing in a developed society: "Look what your materialism has done for you. It has made you soft. You have lost your simplicity, your ability to sacrifice. Your children have turned to drugs and your families are breaking up. I am not against material benefits, but if you are a developed society, I don't want what you have developed into."

God does bless people and prosper them. Hard work, honesty and righteous living result in upward mobility. But baptizing materialism in the name of Jesus, endorsing competition without reckoning with the sinful nature of man, and sanctifying unending economic growth without restraint is not only unbiblical; it has hindered us from serving the urban poor and made our witness a sham in the eyes of those committed to justice in this world. It has robbed many believers of their vision for world evangelization. It has turned scores of evangelical and charismatic churches inward on themselves. Many pastors have lost their passion for the lost. They are still waiting for easy church growth, forgetting that it is God's sovereign blessing and not some spiritual secret that brings people to their churches.

We have forgotten that where *God* is, there is the blessing. His presence is more important than anything we do. Anyplace God visits with His presence is holy, because He is in the midst of the people in that place. He is in the midst of West Indian churches in the big cities of Great Britain. He is in the midst of Italian and Greek communities in the Western suburbs of Melbourne, Australia. He is in the midst of the Maoris in Auckland, New Zealand, and the Turkish guest workers in Frankfurt, West Germany. The city is holy because *God is in the city.*

Many of us are blinded by our cultural prejudices. We think everyone wants to be in a suburb or the countryside. The Chinese culture is an example of a people who do not aspire to rural lifestyles. They feel far more secure and at home when they are crowded close together in a city. God has created all peoples different, and to presume that "our" way is the best way is the worst kind of spiritual and ethnic pride.

Some people love the open countryside, and others get charged up in the city. I love both. I was delighted when a few years ago our children fell in love with the busy humdrum of Amsterdam life. When people asked them if they wanted to live in the countryside, our kids thought they were crazy. They love living in the city.

Even though I grew up fishing and hunting and love the outdoors, if I had to live all my life in a mountain cabin it would be a death sentence. Our family owns a log home in the mountains, and we use it for family retreats, but my heart is in the city. That is where the action is. That is where the people are. I come alive in the city. I love to walk its streets. I love the hustle and bustle, the political activity, the museums and sidewalk cafés. I don't just love the city with the love of the Lord; I like the city. It refuels me to walk its streets.

To me it is just not true that you have to leave the city to get spiritually refreshed. Don't misunderstand me; I need times of rest and retreat like anyone else. But I have no illusions about the countryside being more spiritual than the city. It is God's presence that draws people to Himself, not geography. God is with His people in the city and in the rural areas. He created nature and He created mankind for community. Both are from the Lord, and both can be enjoyed by His people.

Myth Number Two: The City Is Impersonal

Cities can be overwhelming. Riding the underground train in New York, London, Bombay or Paris, or fighting throngs of people in Hong Kong, Los Angeles or Sydney, can be a staggering experience. The same feeling occurs when one drives past street after street of rowhouses and high-rise apartment buildings in any major city in the world. After staying in India for several weeks, my wife described it as "Christmas rush crowds all year long."

Cities bombard people with overwhelming sensory input. Sounds, sights and smells all combine to overload us. For the newcomer to the city this can be a very intimidating experience. It seems too much for any person to handle. Psychological studies have shown that when this occurs people tend to narrow their psychological focus, withdrawing into themselves to shut out unwanted input.

Thus, the New York subway passenger retreats into his own world of reading material or lost thoughts as he rides shoulder to shoulder with a hundred fellow commuters. And the person living in a tiny London flat avoids his nearby neighbors. It is emotional survival.

The perception of the average Christian is that all this sensory input produces mass loneliness. All they can see are millions of faceless people running to and fro, without any human contact. It is not hard to understand why spiritually minded people see this as a negative phenomenon. We worry about city dwellers, wondering if they are hiding in the city and if anyone has ever shared the Gospel with them, much less become personally involved in their lives.

That is the perception, but do we have all the facts? Do our conclusions describe the universal realities, or are they generalizations? In fact, has this view driven us to an unhealthy and unbiblical despair toward the city? Let's take a look at some facts that will help us get a more balanced view of big-city living.

1. *Loneliness is a relative thing.*

Not everyone in the city is lonely. Many people love the big city, and have developed a network of friendships with people of their own language and cultural affinity.

Harvie Conn reminds us that mass migrations from Europe to the United States and Australia in the last century led to the formation of voluntary associations of all kinds. Groups were formed to assist the newcomer on the block with language learning, medical aid, ethnic consciousness, political awareness and church attendance.

Whole neighborhoods of Italian, Greek and Irish people emerged, and in some places still remain. The same is true today of Cambodian and Vietnamese refugees in Paris, Houston and Los Angeles. The return of Pakistanis, Indians and West Indians to England is referred to as the phenomenon of the "empire striking back." And they are not alone. They have formed clubs and associations within their own communities in order to adjust to their new environs.

The fact that crowdedness in the city is perceived as impersonal tells us more about those who feel that way than those who live in the city. White upper-middle-class suburbanites view the city through their own cultural prism. They fail to recognize the differences between cultures. While some see single-family dwellings on lots of open space as natural and necessary, many working class populations and those of different ethnic backgrounds have different desires.

Conn points out that "contact with others is positive, a sign of belonging, not a sign of crowding. Inner-city children are more comfortable being with others than being alone" (p. 45).

2. *Urban life has not produced monolithic loneliness.*

Many people, particularly the poor, enjoy being close to their families and friends. Those who work with urban slum dwellers soon learn that for the poor, joy is found in their friendships; though poor in material things they are rich in relationships.

Christian workers in Manila's "smoky mountain" have been amazed when those who were offered the opportunity to move off the smoldering garbage mountain turned down better living conditions to remain close to their friends.

City-dwelling Europeans may appear to be unfriendly to the American tourist, but Americans are seen as superficial: friendly to everyone, but here today and gone tomorrow. "Cold" European city dwellers take longer to make friends, but their friendships are for life. They may appear to be lonely to the casual observer, but in reality they often have deep friendships that they focus on almost exclusively.

Amsterdam's three hundred or more "brown cafés" are patronized by regulars who obviously enjoy one another's company. They talk openly of their problems to those they know. One bartending couple told me that, though they lost money in their café, they kept it open because they would miss their friends too much if they closed down.

3. *The city is not necessarily anonymous in nature to those who live in it.*

Harvey Cox tells in his book *The Secular City* that many people moved to the city to escape the lack of anonymity they felt forced to assume in the country. They were seeking opportunities to build relationships based on free choice and not forced geographical proximity (p. 43).

In Holland, village life can be quite harsh due to the heavy legalism of hyper-Calvinistic churches that dominate it. In that nation at least, many have moved to the city to find an escape from stifling religious intolerance.

People in high-rise apartments may not know their neighbors, but this does not mean they do not have relationships. They may be living where they are to maintain their privacy, just as farmers in some rural areas don't want to get too "close" to their neighbors—who happen to live three miles down the road!

4. *City life does not cause emotional problems.*

Some sociologists believe the size of the city eats away at mental health, creating "urban malaise"—loneliness, depression and anxiety. An in-depth study of Manhattan residents points the other way:

> Some 1,660 New Yorkers were questioned in the 1950s; 695 of the same group were surveyed again in the 1970s. The results? The mental health of New Yorkers was slightly better than that of the country residents. In fact, the mental health had improved dramatically over the interval between the two samples, especially for women.

A survey taken later by the National Center for Health Statistics reinforced the conclusion. The survey sought to find the incidence of stress-related chronic health problems, such as hypertension and heart disease, among people over sixty-five. It disclosed such problems in 47.8 per 100 farm residents, 47.5 for small-town residents, and 40.5 for city residents.   (Conn, p. 45)

Behavior is not a problem of geography, nor does the city create an impersonal environment, although it can contribute to a person's emotional needs if he does not build meaningful friendships. The city does not induce problems or bring out the worst in people. City is community, and it will reflect what the people make of it themselves, just as a small village can vary in its spiritual makeup according to the character of the people.

Myth Number Three: Cities Are Crime-Ridden and Dangerous

There is crime in the large cities of every Western nation. No one denies this reality, except those involved in breaking the law. But the reaction to crime on the part of Christians is out of all proportion to the facts.

Crime statistics change from neighborhood to neighborhood, and given the large and sprawling nature of our cities, it seems that one must judge each on its own merits.

Further, the definition of crime must also be examined. Certain types of crimes are more prevalent in certain areas, and others are common to all environments. Child abuse, chemical dependency and tax evasion are found everywhere.

White-collar crimes like embezzlement are concentrated in middle-class neighborhoods. If the white-collar criminal were treated with equal harshness in our justice systems the perception that crime is concentrated in the poorer areas of the city would change. The suburbs would be seen to have more than their share of criminal activity.

We tend to define crime in terms of what we perceive to be a threat to our well-being, such as muggings and break-ins. Such limited definitions of crime are overlaid with racial fears. This kind of limited perspective not only produces a myth of suburban safety and inner-city danger, but perpetuates inequality and racism in society.

Many third-world and European cities are much safer than American cities. While certain neighborhoods in European cities do have some physical danger, most are free of violent crimes.

Americans tend to look at all cities through colored glasses. We impute the fear of our cities to all the other cities in the world. Very few societies in the world are as violent as the United States. Perhaps the real problem is that we were birthed as a nation in a violent manner. This violent spirit seems to permeate every aspect of the culture.

In fact, I see no prospect of change in my home nation until there is national repentance over pride in the American Revolution and the violent manner in which the country achieved its nationhood and sovereignty. I think the importance of American independence from the British is more a white middle-class value.

The false perception that violent crime is only an inner-city problem in the United States was exposed in the attack on the Central Park jogger. The gang of youths who went through

Central Park that night "wilding" beat one young finance executive until she was unconscious, but not before brutally raping her. An inner-city crime problem? Follow-up investigations revealed that these were not drug-dependent youths from poor parts of the city: They were bored kids from middle- and upper-income homes out for a "good time." Violence is not the domain of the poor.

Even when there are problems of violence in neighborhoods, the challenge to followers of Christ is one of taking our commitment wholly to follow the Lord Jesus. Did we give our lives totally to Him or not?

In the final analysis, it should make no difference to the true believer if a place is dangerous or not. Our first concern should not be for our own lives. Nor should it be for how much equity we can build up in a house. If you have given your life completely to the Lord Jesus, then it is time to stop complaining and backing out on your commitment. God is looking for those who will give up their rights, lay down their lives and follow Him. Anywhere, anytime. No excuses, no exceptions.

Myth Number Four: The City Is Not a Safe Place to Raise Children

Raising kids is a challenge no matter where it is done. The responsibility of being a good parent is awesome, and not to be taken lightly. Kids face so many pressures growing up that complicating that process by living in a challenging neighborhood seems foolhardy. Or is it?

Granted, raising one's children in an inner-city neighborhood or urban slum area is not easy. To do so requires the grace of God. Having said that, anyone who has a healthy family and a solid relationship with the Lord is a candidate for the Lord's calling. God wants normal people to take up that call. Millions of families are already doing so without the luxury of a choice in the matter.

There is a common Christian myth that has prevented many people from obeying God when it comes to His calling on their families. It goes something like this: To be a good parent I must provide the *best* for my children. They must attend a good Christian school, wear fashionable clothes so their friends will like them, and they must have the best home we can afford in a nice neighborhood.

I challenge that myth for several reasons. Let's look at what is meant by "good" and "bad" neighborhoods. Let's use as an example an upper-middle-class family living in a suburban neighborhood in Orange County, California.

Our exemplary Nice Neighborhood is populated with rather well-to-do, upper-income families headed by hard-working fathers and mothers. They are pleasure-oriented, materialistic and in debt. One or both parents have most likely been divorced and remarried. The family does not attend church, and their teenagers have experimented with drugs and alcohol.

The teens in the family are into pop music, and the fifteen-year-old daughter has already had her first sexual experience. And don't forget the "telly," as my British friends call it. The TV is on five hours a day. Meanwhile the father gives his children three minutes of eye contact a day.

This "average family" faces tremendous pressure to compromise any biblical standards of morality that might have survived thus far. The Nice Neighborhood they live in is filled with the kind of evil that is most dangerous: that which is unseen. They face pressures and temptations daily to bow before the gods of materialism and pleasure. Their friends have more than they do, and they are racing madly to keep up. They live for themselves, and though they may be *nice people* living in a *nice neighborhood,* they are separated from Christ and are part of a culture that not only condones their lifestyle, but deifies it.

The Bible speaks clearly about idolatry. God does not see this as a nice neighborhood; this is a dangerous neighborhood. The families that live here have it all the more difficult because the evil that surrounds them looks so good.

I challenge the myth of the good and bad neighborhoods because I do not agree with its basic presuppositions. For most people *good* and *bad* are defined by safety and comfort. A good neighborhood has no "problems" or physical challenges. All the people are "clean" and "neat."

These are not biblical standards. Deciding where we live and how we see people should be based on values different from the rest of society. The Kingdom of God is not food and drink. In fact, neighborhoods and cities are judged in the Bible by their disobedience or obedience to God. We ought to do the same.

Living by biblical standards will create a spiritual momentum for our families that will keep us on our toes. It will put us on the offensive in our relationship with God, making it imperative that we spend time in prayer and spiritual warfare as a family. Our children will have a heritage of compassion, justice and evangelism. We will pass on biblical values to our children that are forged in the furnace of Christian service. What better gift could we give them?

As I mentioned earlier my family lives on the edge of the

red light district of Amsterdam. Here the dangers are certainly not hidden. Thousands of prostitutes ply their wares on the streets and sit behind picture windows in small rooms along the canals. There are porn shops and sex clubs everywhere. Many people have AIDS. There are hundreds of hard drug users. If you walk down the wrong alley at the wrong time of day, you will be relieved of your wallet and pocket change in short order.

We first moved to Amsterdam in 1973, and in 1980, when our children were five and seven years old, we moved into the red light district. We do not live here because we must, but because it is a privilege. We made the choice with our kids prayerfully, and have reviewed it with them regularly through the years. None of us has any regrets. We all love the city and celebrate its life daily. The Lord has enabled us by His grace to fulfill His calling with joy. We faced the myth that the city is not a "nice" place to live as a family and found it held no power or validity.

Myth Number Five: The City Cannot Be Changed

To dissect this myth we must examine the problem of power and how it affects people. Some people have power in the city; many don't. Powerlessness means other people control your life. For those who do not have power, the effects can be devastating.

Most Western Christians have no idea what powerlessness means. They have never experienced it, and have not dared to enter the world of those who do. The closest a person of means ever comes to this agonizing state is to be audited by the tax authorities or accused unjustly of a crime they did not commit. Even then they can fight back because they have the means and the contacts to do so. They have the will to fight back because they have dignity and resources. When one loses those things, all is lost.

Cities become the power centers in the modern world of communication, information, finance and government. But for most people, this means manipulation and injustice. For the black person living in a section of the city that banks have decided to "red zone" (where the risks are considered too great to grant personal or small business loans), a loan under normal circumstances is impossible.

Harvie Conn calls this the "urban tower power" syndrome and traces its roots back to the tower of Babel. Though God planned for people to live in city communities for His purposes, some rebelled and turned the city into a place to make their own names great. Cities have been spiritual battlefields ever since for those who stand against the Lordship of Christ. Evil men and women have sought to turn cities into power centers of greed and corruption.

The prophets called those who failed to fulfill God's purpose in the city to account for their betrayal of God's glory (see Isaiah 47; Jeremiah 50; Habbakuk 1; Amos 1–3). The writer of the book of Revelation warns of impending doom to Babylon the great for her harlotries: "Alas! alas! thou great city, thou mighty city, Babylon!" (Revelation 18:10, 16, 19).

The cities of our world often look like war zones. There is physical destruction and spiritual despair. Decades of welfare programs have not turned the tide, nor has the recent bent toward conservative economic policies. Because cities have a spiritual dimension, they will be changed only by those who perceive the spiritual nature of the battle and exercise true spiritual authority.

This does not mean that working toward social programs and standing for justice in the city is not important. Quite the contrary, cities will not be changed without those who are willing to lay down their lives for people in need. But at the heart of the matter lies a spiritual battle, and godly men and women are needed who will fight it.

If Christians are to take seriously the call to overcome evil in the city, there must be changes in the following four areas:

1. *We must approach the city with faith that God can change the urban power structures.*

God's sovereign power is great enough to change the most wicked city. When I first moved to Amsterdam, I was overwhelmed by the vast numbers of unchurched people and the unbelievable immorality. I learned that less than two percent of greater Amsterdam's population of one-and-a-half million people attended church, and that it was the single largest supplier of child pornography to the United States, shipping more than one billion dollars' worth a year through its postal system.

It was when I started meditating on the book of Jonah that my unbelief was challenged. I recognized that I had become more impressed with the power of evil in the city than I was with God's power to change the city. God used a rebellious prophet to bring "that great city" to its knees (Jonah 4:11). I decided that if God could do it for Nineveh, He could do it again. Those who wield power do respond to God's grace. Harvie Conn points to other biblical examples of change:

> A fifty-five-year reign—a trail of power highlighted by pride, child sacrifice, and syncretistic animism—ended

with repentant Manasseh restored (2 Chronicles 33:1–13). Nebuchadnezzar, who boasted of "Babylon the great" built by his own hand for the glory of his majesty (Daniel 4:30), turned from self-praise to "exalt and honor the King of heaven" (Daniel 4:37). Ephesus, the most important city in the Roman province of Asia, was shaken by a movement to Christ among the religious power brokers. . . . The powerful in the world of animism discarded the secret names with secret authority in order to magnify another power name, the Lord Jesus (Acts 19:17). (p. 167)

2. *We must repent of our urban prejudices and be willing to do anything God asks of us to serve in the city.*

Turning our backs on neighborhoods because of their ethnic and economic constituency is a deeply ingrained pattern that goes back to the last century. It is taken for granted but rooted in prejudice and fear.

The reaction was set in motion when we fled from neighborhoods being "invaded" by Greeks in Australia, Irish and blacks in the United States, and Pakistanis and West Indians in the U.K. Whole subcultures and suburbs were born out of this flight pattern. Those who were too poor to run stayed and fought it out, contesting control for their neighborhoods in political power struggles.

Where was the Gospel in all this? This is precisely the question that must be faced. Instead of seeing God's hand in answering our missionary prayers and bringing the people of the world to our doorstep, we reacted in anger over the supposed violation of our rights to live in neighborhoods that we did not want invaded by "outsiders." Christians did not shape how society responded to this phenomenon, but followed the lead of the ungodly.

It is time to turn the tide. When we truly understand the devastation that this abandonment has brought, I believe it will produce repentance in those who are serious about serving God.

3. *It is time to return to the city.*

We must return, not as developers to change the city into our image and make a nice profit as we do so, but as servants to help others by our presence and to use our resources to rise above those things that make them powerless.

I hesitate to call for a massive move to cities with challenges that many of us are not prepared to cope with. Cambodian, Pakistani, Hispanic and Samoan suburbs are not crying out for white do-gooders to invade them. But servants, learners, friends—these are needed and welcomed.

We all want genuine friends who have time to listen, who will care enough to understand and respond in a sensitive manner. In most situations this will mean a cross-cultural experience. We will be confronted with different value systems, different thinking processes, different ways of viewing time and its importance. Our whole framework for evaluating the meaning of our lives will be shaken. If you are prepared for that kind of experience and willing to learn and grow through the encounter, then you are a candidate for God's call to the city.

4. *Real authority does not come from ruling over someone, but from serving beside him or her as a friend.*

We are quick to pronounce what other people's problems are, then impose our own solutions. This does not empower the poor, but enslaves them to one more set of dependent relationships.

Power comes when we give it away to others. Our respect for the poorest of the poor, our belief that they have much to teach us, our acknowledgment that we do not understand the problems they face and the solutions they need are the first steps in bringing dignity to those who have been patronized and used in the city. Our faith in Jesus Christ will be rejected by some of those we serve. And not only will they reject Him, but some of them will turn against us as well, using the very resources we helped create for them to do so.

Jesus faced this dilemma and chose to embrace the ultimate rejection of those He came to save. He forgave them, endured the cross and overcame their rejection through obedience to His Father. His example is ours. He gave up His rights, His power, but in doing so was granted a new level of spiritual authority. Many have been made righteous because of His obedience.

May God grant us the grace to lay down our lives for others, just as He did for us.

Part 3
The Church in the City

6
Incarnational Presence

She arrived in Paris in 1881 at the age of 21. She was accompanied by two teenage friends, and they set out to turn the city on its ear. They could not have arrived at a more turbulent time: crime, disease, alcoholism and violent anti-clericalism were rampant. It was a veritable Sodom. These were the early days of the Third Republic and bitter memories of the commune lingered on.

One of the first things Catherine Booth and her fearless band learned to do was to *pin* on their bonnet strings rather than sew them on. This was more practical considering that when they went into the bars and cafés to preach, men would grab their bonnet strings from behind and try to strangle them.

Obviously, the Parisians were not receptive to the Gospel! Huge cobblestones were hurled into the young women's meetings, and they suffered physical and verbal abuse. By the fifth anniversary of the Salvation Army in Paris, two hundred of its soldiers had been injured, 175 arrested, and one killed.

Young Catherine Booth never flinched. She had given her first sermon at the age of fourteen, and when asked about her favorite passage of the Bible, she shared her love for the story of Christ's death. When she arrived in Paris, she was dubbed *la Capitaine*. Within eight months, and for the rest of her life, she was *la Maréchale*, the Field Marshal.

She was resented by the French for her clothes, her accent and her optimism, but in the end they came to respect and love her dearly. She was paid the highest compliment given by the French: "She loves France" (*International Herald Tribune*, August 15, 1981).

Even when they fought her they admired her bold style and courage. From the beginning she refused to use an interpreter: "If I begin with crutches I shall always need crutches." One hundred years after she arrived in France she was still honored. Articles, books and special celebrations marked the anniversary of the coming of *la Maréchale*.

Why was she loved so dearly? Certainly the impact her preaching had on Parisian society was not small, with thousands coming to Christ through her ministry. Just as important was the depth of her care for the poor. She showed love and respect for every person she met. But above all else was her desire to become French to the French. She won their hearts by becoming one of them.

Fleshing Out the Gospel

Young Catherine followed the example of her Lord by being among the people. She understood that at the heart of the Gospel was the fact that Jesus came; He actually lived among the very people He came to reach. By immersing themselves in French culture and by loving the French people with total commitment, Catherine and her team created an incarnational presence. They not only declared the Gospel with their words; they demonstrated it with their lives.

John 1:14 says of Jesus: "And the Word became flesh and dwelt among us, full of grace and truth; we have beheld his glory. . . ." Further, Jesus said to His disciples toward the end of His earthly ministry, "As the Father has sent me, even so I send you" (20:21). Jesus was concerned that the disciples go into all the world in the same manner in which He came—in humility, living among the people as one of them.

God did not send His Son in a fiery chariot, riding above the masses, shouting messages of prophetic warning. Jesus was one with people. He was born in simplicity and raised in obscurity. His mother's reputation was questionable among her neighbors and His father died when He was a youth. He spoke the language of the common man and learned a trade.

God did not remain aloof from our problems, but entered into them by becoming a man and living a normal life. His authority is rooted not only in who He is, but also in the fact that the Creator stepped into His creation.

The coming of the Lord Jesus Christ as servant of man and Son of God is not only God's way of reconciling His creation to Himself; it is also a demonstration of how we should act in a fallen world. It is not only the means by which God offers salvation to the world; it is the model for the Church to follow as she lives and serves in the city.

The Church in the City

Christian presence that is divorced from the example of the Lord Jesus is not Christian. No matter what our words, if we do not follow the example of His servanthood our lives deny the truth of what we say. Truth is lived and spoken. Authority to speak about people's lives comes from our commitment to live among them as servants.

This is why television and radio evangelism ministries can quickly undermine their own calling. Those who minister through these media can create an impression of personalness that is impossible to live out. When a person on TV says, "It is good to be with you today in your living room," or, "I am praying for *you* right now," he is not only speaking a lie but shortcutting the way God has instructed us to serve those who are in need.

This does not mean that we cannot use these media to communicate the Gospel, but it does mean that our responsibility to do so ethically is under greater pressure. There is no substitute for the presence of the local church, demonstrating the Gospel by living, working and rubbing shoulders with skeptical pagans. Our corporate presence as the Body of Christ is just that—we are the Body of Christ. Not in a mystical sense, nor are we deity, but God has chosen to reveal Himself through the Church. In the Old Testament He dwelt in a special way in a tabernacle. When Christ came He dwelt in a human body. Now the whole Church is His Body, the meeting place between God and man.

When the local church fails to *be* the Gospel, our witness is no longer viable. But when we are all that God intend-

106

ed us to be, the Church becomes a powerful witness to Christ.

It is possible to be a Christian and not be an incarnational Christian. It is also possible to commit ourselves to follow Christ and yet never truly live among people as one who is called to serve. We can start the journey without completing it. The incarnational model of the Lord Jesus not only compels us to accept Christ as our Savior, but demands that we leave behind our cultural baggage, our rights and our attachments to citizenship in earthly kingdoms.

This truth does not just apply to missionaries. It is at the heart of the Christian life for all believers. Every major decision we make in life as individuals and as congregations should be made in the light of Christ's incarnation. When we are offered better jobs, do we ask ourselves if it will help us be more like Jesus, help serve His purposes on earth? Or do we assume that if there is more pay involved, God is blessing us and, therefore, it is automatically His will to accept the new position? Are we more concerned about being upwardly mobile than serving those in need around us? Are we bent on getting ahead or getting where God is sending us? The two directions need not be incompatible but often are.

Jesus lived among us so that we would know reality. He endured the shame and pain of the cross, He went through the misunderstandings, He experienced the mundaneness of our lives, waited patiently 33 years and gave the ultimate sacrifice so that we would be reconciled to the Father.

And He has called us to do the same. To follow His example, believers will embrace the challenge to get involved in people's lives. Building relationships with those who do not know Christ will be our consuming passion and will take precedence over seeking pleasure for ourselves.

Jesus' Example: Listening and Caring

You might say that Jesus spent thirty years listening and three years speaking. Or as one Japanese evangelist put it, "We have twice as many ears as mouths, so we should spend twice as much time listening as we do talking."

Jesus did not just hear words, but hearts. He really listened. He stopped at the well at noontime to converse with a Samaritan woman. He took the little children in His arms and talked to them, listening intently as they chattered away. He went out of His way to be with people. This kind of listening takes time. It means interrupting our plans. It means feeling what others feel and weeping when they weep, not just so we can win them to our cause but because we genuinely care.

Listening means *understanding*. No one likes to be patronized or talked down to. We want to know that we are understood and respected. Without it we don't feel secure in opening up our hearts to someone.

Listening means *acceptance*. Not that we want someone to agree with us all the time, but we appreciate it when a person has the ability to see our failures and to love us unconditionally. Deep inside we all know that acceptance does not mean agreement, but that a person is committed to us no matter how badly we blow it.

Listening means respect. We dignify the lives of others by taking seriously the expression of their likes and dislikes, their dreams and doubts, their joys and sorrows. Every person is created in the image of God and, therefore, has great worth.

Every aspiration, every decision has great value, whether or not it is consistent with the Christian faith. When we allow a person's status in life—his poverty or wealth, political or moral views—to block our respect for his basic humanity, we have communicated by our attitude that we do not take him seriously; we do not respect him.

Jesus was able to transcend the fallenness of those He lived with and show them He cared for them as people. In spite of His awesome holiness and infinite power, Jesus demonstrated His commitment to listen and care for Samaritans and women, prostitutes and tax collectors, children and indeed anyone whom society counted as of little worth; they were of great importance to Him. This is what the incarnation was all about.

Unfortunately, many Christians have not demonstrated this same willingness or ability. By our attitudes toward non-Christians we actually communicate just the opposite of what our Lord did. Many evangelicals have allowed Christianity to become a religion, something more important than people. They make doctrine more important than being like Jesus, and substitute trust in creeds and confessions for their trust in Christ. They are in danger of creating a Christianity in their own image and falling down and worshiping themselves.

Jesus, the Creator of the universe, the Lamb of God, chose to become a servant. He accepted slander and abuse, bitterness and rejection, because He chose another way. He chose the way of the cross because it was the way to our hearts. He did not want a kingdom of slaves who served Him because they had to, but an army of love-slaves whose loyalty was won by the love of their Master.

It was for this reason that He performed mighty deeds; He was intent on loving people into the Kingdom. He was moved with compassion by the needs of His creation and responded out of His great love to heal them. It was not sympathy that motivated Him, nor was it a fascination with His divine power. He had no need to prove He was a man of great faith. He simply loved people.

It was this love that sent Jesus into the world: "For God so loved the world . . ." (John 3:16). And it is the same love that will thrust us into the world. When His love fills our hearts it will compel us to lay down our lives, to give up our rights and to serve others, even till death if necessary.

Jesus said to His disciples, "As the Father has sent me, even so I send you" (John 20:21). This commission is ours; it is not for a small group of men who lived long ago. The world is our home. *We* are the sent ones.

The incarnation is our example, our model for life and for mission. And as God's people it is our guiding light for the city. Not only is the city created and loved by God; it is our place of calling and service for local congregations. For those who grasp the goodness of God in allowing them this privilege, the city is our sacred place, the place of our opportunity to follow the example of our Lord.

For those congregations who embrace the example of the Lord Jesus as their model for corporate church life, the city will more often than not be the place to go, our home while sojourning until we reach our lasting home. It is the place to live out the Gospel as servants, laying down our lives so that others may find life.

7
Apostles to the City

The young couple sitting before me poured out their hearts. They were incensed by the idolatry they saw around them. They explained they had had a missionary calling to the nation of India. When they arrived, they were shocked at the vast number of idols that people worshiped in this strange and fascinating land.

They had read about Hinduism, but when they saw it being lived out before their eyes, when they visited the Hindu temples, saw the monkey gods and experienced Indian people actually bowing before graven images, it made them angry.

They explained their plan. They wanted to go onto the streets, to the temples and the homes of Hindu priests, and explain what the Bible said about idolatry. They felt they should warn the people of God's judgment to come.

This all sounded very well. But something was missing. I asked them three simple questions: "I understand how important it is for us to speak about idolatry from a biblical perspective, but before you do that let me ask you some questions. First, can you assure me that you have some Indian friends who are non-Christians that you know by name, who have been in your home and you in theirs, and whom you like as people?"

The couple sat with a puzzled look for a time. Silence ensued as they tried to remember the name of someone they might have met on a street corner and had a cup of tea with. "No, not really, but we plan to do that. We've only been here eight months. . . ."

Next question: "Well, then, can you tell me three or four things about this culture that you deeply appreciate and have come to respect?"

Again a puzzled look, the eyebrows raised and the foreheads furrowed in deep thought. "Why, no, of course not. Can't you see? This country is ruled by demon spirits. It's totally demonic. Everything about the country has been destroyed by Hinduism. Can't you see that?"

I went on to the third question. "You have been here eight months; you've had enough time to experience the culture, to meet people, to see the needs of this land. Have you fasted? Have you lost sleep because of the burden of prayer on your hearts for this land? Have you wept for India?"

The silence this time was indeed embarrassing.

With great sadness in my heart I explained that they had no authority to preach the Gospel in India. Until they saw the good in the culture, until they knew Indians personally and were having social and friendship needs met through them, and until they were brokenhearted with a deep love for the people, they would never have the right to preach the Gospel to Indians or to lift a finger in even a gentle rebuke about the idolatry of the land.

Seeing through God's Eyes

Authority to preach the Gospel and minister in the name of Jesus Christ in a city or nation is gained not just by being called by God, but by fulfilling the conditions of that call.

When I came to the city of Amsterdam I spent six months simply walking the streets of every major neighborhood in the city. I rode trams and metros and buses, getting a feel for the city. I asked God to let me see the city through His eyes. I asked Him to help me understand her culture. I read every book I could get my hands on about Amsterdam. I sat in coffee shops and "brown cafés," listening to the people. I developed a fondness for the openhearted, humor-loving, sea-faring Amsterdamer.

It was out of those many months of walking her streets that I grew to love the city of Amsterdam. In fact, now I not only love her, I like her!

There is a perception that the Bible is an anti-urban Book. People seek justification for their urban racism: "David, after all, was a shepherd." This prejudice is not rooted in God's heart, and the Bible makes that abundantly clear. There are more than 1,400 references to cities in the Bible, many expressing God's love and concern for the people in and around her. Of these, I have chosen four men and four cities to examine in a closer way. They serve as models for the Church's mission to the city today.

Nehemiah and Jerusalem

The Church's involvement in cities must include a commitment to rebuilding the city's social, familial, educational, medical and economic support systems. This commitment to urban community development needs to include a wide range of activities that embrace everything from prophetic denunciation of injustice, musical presentations of the Gospel, counselors to care for the wounded, professional workers to help with training and the rebuilding of the community, elections putting the godly in roles of government to ensure that corruption is uprooted and righteousness is upheld, and evangelism and church planting.

This all-encompassing approach to community development is spelled out by Roger Greenway in his book *Apostles to the City*:

> Nehemiah, the architect of Jerusalem's urban renewal, had something very special in mind for this day . . . the returned exiles from Babylon gathered at the Water Gate of the temple in Jerusalem. They were celebrating the Feast of Trumpets, a sacred festival that God had ordained as an annual celebration on the first day of the seventh month. . . . He had put forward every effort to inspire the people to rebuild the ruined city. They had cleared away the rubble, erected the walls, and built new houses. It had been a tremendous undertaking and Nehemiah was proud of the people's accomplishments. But something more was needed. Nehemiah realized that moral and religious reforms had to be made to give the nation a spiritual foundation that would set it apart from other nations and prevent the kind of decay that had

114

precipitated its former destruction. For social and political reforms to take hold in a way that would please God
and preserve the people, spiritual renewal must occur.
This could happen only if God's word was known, understood and obeyed.   (p. 45)

Following are principles from the book of Nehemiah that
apply specifically to community development in an urban context. It is important to note that practical and spiritual dimensions are integrated in the book of Nehemiah. It is at the same
time a book of leadership principles, teaching on spiritual
warfare, practical guidelines to urban renewal and the importance of justice and righteousness.

1. *We learn from the book of Nehemiah that urban community
development should be birthed in intercession, fasting and confession
of sin.*

Nehemiah heard a report about the sins of the people of
Israel and, in a wonderful act of identification, confessed those
sins as his own. "We have sinned against thee" (Nehemiah
1:6). Seeing the conditions of cities should drive us to our
knees in deep sorrow and grief. Anger toward the injustice of
those who have destroyed the city must affect us to the point
that we identify with the selfishness that has caused the problems; otherwise, there can be no weeping and mourning.

It is important to note, further, that it was in the place of
prayer that Nehemiah received inspiration and direction from
the Lord on how to be involved personally in the rebuilding of
Jerusalem. Action without prayer is only human enthusiasm;
action born out of prayer is divine inspiration and direction.

Nehemiah used the power structures of the day for the
benefit of his people. He did not set himself on a collision

course with the non-Jewish king that he served, but rather he appealed for his help and cooperation in rebuilding the walls of Jerusalem.

Rather than treating governmental structures as our enemies, we should seek every way possible to find their cooperation and their goodwill (Nehemiah 2:2–3, 6). Obviously there are times when we will be on a collision course with corrupt officials and uncooperative power structures, but every effort should be given to win their favor. When that does not happen, the Bible speaks to the importance of exposing and resisting unjust power structures.

2. *Nehemiah took the time to understand the needs of Jerusalem.*

Too often development work is done on the spur of the moment. Long-term development projects must take over where disaster relief finishes. There is no excuse for a lack of thorough research and preparation for the projects we take on. Nehemiah inspected the walls of Jerusalem in order to know exactly what the needs were (Nehemiah 2:11–16).

3. *Spiritual opposition in the form of criticism, mockery, attempted bribery and physical threats should be expected when we are involved in urban community development.*

Community development is a spiritual task. Seeking to meet the physical, emotional, mental and spiritual needs of any people will bring a swift retaliation from spiritual powers that seek to destroy people's lives.

We must study God's Word carefully to understand the spiritual dimension of power encounters, and understand the weapons and authority that are at our disposal as believers. The Bible makes it clear that our weapons are not carnal but spiritual. We must learn to respond in the spirit opposite to that of our enemies if we are to win spiritual battles. Here are examples:

- When Nehemiah was criticized by Sanballat and To-biah, his response was to pray and keep working (Ne-hemiah 4:1–6).
- When Nehemiah was threatened with physical abuse, he set armed guards to watch over their property and protect the people (Nehemiah 4:7–9).
- When the people became afraid, Nehemiah spent time strengthening and encouraging them, as well as renewing the weak portions in the wall (Nehemiah 4:13–14).
- When the people were separated from each other and vulnerable to attack, Nehemiah established a communications system so that they could support one another (Nehemiah 4:19–20).
- Nehemiah took practical precautions and taught the people basic survival skills (Nehemiah 4:21–23).
- When Nehemiah learned that there was economic injustice within the community of Jewish believers, and that some of the people were exploiting others unjustly, he became angry. He exposed the corruption and brought charges against those who were involved. He held a public assembly and righted the wrongs that had been done. He participated personally in rectifying the economic situations by using his own financial resources to do all that he could to make things right. Nehemiah was not afraid to confront corruption, injustice and economic unrighteousness within the congregation of the people. This won the trust of the people

117

and allowed them to work in peace and harmony (Nehemiah 5:6–13).

- Nehemiah lived a restrained lifestyle and modeled before the people an example of economic frugality. This prevented him from being open to any charge from his enemies that he was exploiting the people for selfish gain (Nehemiah 5:14–15).
- When Nehemiah was lured into a trap by his enemies, he refused to be engaged with fruitless discussions with people who were opposed to the work of God. He would not meet with Sanballat and Tobiah (Nehemiah 6:1–3).
- When Sanballat sought to manipulate Nehemiah through attacks on his reputation, Nehemiah did not give in to the demands of his enemies. He answered them truthfully by declaring the facts, but he realized that the motive of his enemies was to strike fear into his heart. He turned to God for help, recognizing that the battle was the Lord's (Nehemiah 6:7–9).
- When Nehemiah discerned false prophets were coming against him to prophesy threats and warnings, he would not compromise himself in any way to their attacks (Nehemiah 6:10–14).

4. *Nehemiah understood the importance of teaching God's law and proclaiming God's Word in urban renewal.*

He insisted on reading the Word of God publicly and called the people to account for how they were living. He was not a man who ignored the spiritual dimensions of the people at the price of caring for them physically. He encouraged a revival movement that was rooted in repentance and public restitution. He asked for the resumption of worship and delegated this responsibility to those who were anointed for the task (Nehemiah 9:1–8, 32–38).

5. *Nehemiah lived among the people he was called to serve.*

It is impossible to serve people meaningfully in a community development project without doing so (Nehemiah 11:1–2). Though this is impossible in some situations, every effort must be made to live as close to the people as possible.

6. *Nehemiah had a holistic view of community development that integrated worship and celebration in the urban renewal process.*

All too often people have a narrow view of community development. They think of job training, political lobbying and feeding the poor. Celebrations of worship must also be a part of the process. Nehemiah was not afraid to encourage the people to celebrate. At one point there was so much sadness in the camp over the revelation of their sins, Nehemiah declared a love feast and asked the people to stop mourning so they might receive the grace of God (Nehemiah 8:9–12).

7. *Nehemiah stood against false prophets, false teachers and ungodly priests who were corrupting the city.*

Today the inner cities need a revival among those who are exploiting black and Asian churches and using them for their own gain. False priests need to be confronted with their sins. The Church must cleanse itself.

The work on the wall in Jerusalem was completed in 52 days. God blessed the work of Nehemiah's hands because he was a man of integrity and courage. His balance is an example to all those who wish to be involved in the city. His prayer should become ours as well:

> Thus I cleansed them from everything foreign, and I
> established the duties of the priests and Levites, each in

his work; and I provided for the wood offering, at appointed times, and for the first fruits. Remember me, O my God, for good.

Nehemiah 13:30–31

Jonah and Nineveh

After walking the streets of Amsterdam for six months I was overwhelmed. I passed block after block of rowhouses. I walked through high-rise apartment complexes with buildings hundreds of yards long that housed up to 1,500 people per building. I saw slum areas that were poverty-stricken, neighborhoods that were rundown. I passed hundreds of thousands of people who did not know Jesus Christ. My research had shown me that there were eight or nine evangelical churches in the city of Amsterdam. Church attendance was less than two percent; I was told that one-tenth of one percent of the population in the city was committed to Christianity, though, of course, no one could really say for sure.

I learned that Amsterdam was the sex capital of Europe, and that forty to fifty thousand homosexuals visited Amsterdam every weekend. I saw with my own eyes, as I have mentioned, the sex clubs and the child pornography. I saw hawkers standing in front of theaters calling people to watch live sex acts. I saw advertisements in magazines placed by the Board of Tourism proudly proclaiming the pleasure of Amsterdam's "world-renowned red-light district."

I experienced a city with a restive political atmosphere and a leftist youth movement that was deeply concerned about world problems, such as apartheid and nuclear armaments. I visited vandalized apartment buildings that young people had broken into and turned into their squat houses. I heard the passion of these young people as they spoke of economic injustice and the unfairness of rich landlords holding onto their empty buildings to push up rental prices in the free sector of the economy.

I saw no hope for the city of Amsterdam. Until I read the book of Jonah.

It was in this little book that I rediscovered how God used a proud prophet to turn around one of the most wicked cities in the history of mankind. Nineveh had reigned for 1,500 years as a ruthless city-state without being defeated by another military power. Traces of at least two walls around the city have been found. They are wide enough to drive three cars side by side. Some archaeologists estimate that eleven different walls surrounded the city.

We know from reading the book of Jonah that it took three days to walk across the city (Jonah 3). Nineveh was famous for her military power and cruelty to her foes. It took 12,000 slaves ten years to build the king's palace. Her temples were famous for prostitution.

Nineveh was the capital of Syria, Israel's archenemies to the north. They often invaded villages on the northern border of Israel and thus were hated by the people of God. It is no wonder that Jonah resisted the call of God to go and proclaim not only the Lord's judgment but His salvation to the people of Nineveh.

If ever there was a picture of the Church in today's world, it is painted for us in the opening verses of this little book. God spoke to the prophet and called him to the city. Jonah was alarmed and ran the other way. He went to the port, bought a ticket and headed for Tarshish. While on the boat a great storm arose, and Jonah slept while Nineveh went to hell. Here is what we learn for today's churches.

1. *We learn in this book that God loves cities.*

Not only did He love the Nineveh that He called Jonah to, but He loves the Ninevehs of our world. He loves Liverpool and London, He loves Lagos and Bangkok, He loves San Francisco and Washington, D.C. The question we must ask is this: Do we love cities the way God does? Are we more like Jonah in his reaction to the city of Nineveh, or are we like the Lord in His commitment to people?

2. *Certain cities are strategic in God's purposes.*

God focused His attention on the city of Nineveh not only because it was a source of great evil influence, but because it was also to be a source of great blessing. He chose Nineveh because He wanted to make it an example of righteousness. A revival broke out in Nineveh that swept the entire city, from the king to the most common laborer. What an impact this must have had on the villages around it! And yet it seems the revival was cut short because of Jonah's reaction. What would have happened if the prophet had responded differently?

3. *God uses weak human beings.*

When I first read this book of Jonah I was encouraged. I thought to myself, *If God can use Jonah, He can use me!* Have you ever said, "God can't use me; I don't have theological training," or, "I can't do it; I'm not as gifted as this person or that person"?

It is the weak people of the world who confound the mighty. It is the very fact that we know we cannot do something that gives us our greatest qualification—if we call upon the Lord. Do not be more taken with the evil of the city than with the greatness of God. His greatness through you can make a mighty difference.

4. *God uses the simplicity of preaching.*

What a powerful lesson! And yet it is so often overlooked by the Church. At the very heart of all mission work, at the heart of all concern for poor, must be the proclamation of the Good News of Jesus Christ, whether it is done through drama, music, medical work, community development or church planting. Everything we do must be centered around Christ.

5. *There is hope for cities.*

In his book *The Meaning of the City* Jacques Ellul reaches the conclusion that cities are held under the sway of principalities and powers. Pessimism comes through Ellul's book, particularly in the contrast he draws between the city of God and the city of man. Though Ellul's point is well taken, that humankind seeks to create a false alternative community in the city as a result of their rebellion against God, we must not forget that it was God who put the longing for community, for city and togetherness, in man's heart in the beginning.

Going further than Ellul, many sociologists are overwhelmed by the problems of fallen mankind when brought to focus in the city. But rather than join in this pessimism, it is important to remember that God ordained the city, and that when man lives by God's precepts the city will be redeemed: "When it goes well with the righteous, the city rejoices" (Proverbs 11:10).

Further, the revival and redemption of a city like Nineveh encourage us that no city is beyond God's redemption.

It is a warning to all those who bear the name of Christ that God intends to be at work in the city whether we cooperate with Him or not. His sovereign will shall be done. Men and women will seek Him and find Him. He will redeem peoples, neighborhoods and cities. The question is, Will we be on the outside of what God is doing, like Jonah, looking on, or will we be in the middle of God's redemptive acts in the city?

An Unknown Layman and Antioch

Antioch was the first city to have a Gentile congregation. It was the first city in which the Church sent out missionaries. That was the first church to send financial relief to another church. And it was the first city in which the followers of Christ had the wonderful distinction of being called "Christians."

This magnificent city was located on the Orontes River, and was the capital of the Roman province of Syria—the third most important city in the Roman Empire. It was a multiracial, militaristic, idolatrous, wealthy, sex-mad city. In one word, it was "modern."

Interestingly, the church at Antioch had some of the most colorful experiences recorded in the Bible. It was in Antioch that Paul confronted Peter face to face, and it was there that the controversy over circumcision arose.

According to Charles Ludwig in his book *Cities in New Testament Times*, the site for the founding of Antioch was selected by Alexander the Great. After he had defeated the Persian king, Darius III, Alexander marched south where he began a seven-month-long siege of the city of Tyre. He stopped just east of the city, where he drank from a spring. The water was so sweet and refreshing that he decided to build a city on the spot:

Eventually, Seleucus—one of Alexander's generals—became the ruler of Syria. Burning with a passion to perpetuate the name of his father Antiochus, Seleucus founded and named the . . . city after him.　　(p. 78)

The church in Antioch became a great spiritual power-house. Many have modeled church life after it. Although that church was led by such great men as Paul and Barnabas, it was actually started by an unknown layman fleeing persecution in the city of Jerusalem. Acts 11:19–21 says:

Now those who were scattered because of the persecution that arose over Stephen traveled as far as Phoenicia and Cyprus and Antioch, speaking the word to none except Jews. But there were some of them, men of Cyprus and Cyrene, who on coming to Antioch spoke to the Greeks also, preaching the Lord Jesus. And the hand of the Lord was with them, and a great number that believed turned to the Lord.

When news of this growth reached Jerusalem, church leaders there sent Barnabas to Antioch. He saw the grace of the Lord upon the church and rejoiced with them. Under Barnabas' leadership a large company was added to the church. Barnabas went to Tarsus to look for Paul and brought him back with him to Antioch to help lead the blossoming work of God in the city.

Many have wondered at the strength and the impact the church had upon the city of Antioch. What was the secret of its growth and its spiritual power? Seven things stand out that can teach us about church life in the city.

1. *The power of fellowship.*

The church in Antioch was a multiracial fellowship made up of Africans, Europeans and Asians. Both Jew and Gentile worshiped together in harmony.

If the churches today are to make an impact upon the cities of our modern world, we too must break across the racial barriers and the cultural dividers in society. The Church has to demonstrate that she has the power to bring all classes together. Although we may grow more quickly along cultural and ethnic lines, we must never allow those lines to become walls. If we want power, there must be unity and that unity must be a demonstration that that which divides society will never divide the Church.

2. *The power of team leadership.*

When Barnabas brought Saul to Antioch, he initiated a God-designed plan for leadership in the church. Barnabas realized that he could not lead the church alone; he needed help. Eventually that leadership team grew to include prophets, teachers, evangelists and apostles as well as pastors. It was a well-rounded group whose gifts complemented one another.

This kind of plurality always needs a "senior among equals." Equality does not mean that we do not recognize those with senior maturity or anointing. Nor does it mean that we do not recognize a need for orderly authority in our midst. If we are to have a growing and stable fellowship, we need to have a team of men and women with varieties of gifts and personalities that holds one another accountable and provides balance and direction to the body it serves.

3. *The power of every-member ministry.*

When we read about the church in Antioch we read about a church that encouraged members to be involved in the ministry. The leaders were seen as equippers, the people as ministers. It was a layperson who started the church and it was ordinary people by their witness in the shops and in the marketplaces who became known as the followers of Christ: Christians.

4. *The power of teaching.*

Acts 13:1 says that there were "prophets and teachers, Barnabas, Symeon. . . ." We can never underestimate the power of teaching God's Word. The authoritative proclamation of the eternal truths of Scripture makes a powerful impact on people. The result is that the Church grows in spiritual maturity and in number. The church in Antioch was taught the ways of God. New Christians were taught how to be faithful to their Master, and leaders were taught how to equip the saints and minister faithfully to the people of God.

5. *The power of worship and prayer.*

It is a fascinating insight into early Church life to see the leadership team in Antioch meeting together for a time of fasting and worship (Acts 13:1–3). It was during this time that the Holy Spirit told them to set aside Barnabas and Paul for missionary work.

This points to the fact that they did not follow a static form of worship, controlled by presettable liturgy with no opportunity for the Holy Spirit to speak. They were able to hear from the Lord and His response to their petitions.

If the Church of Jesus Christ is to be all that she is intended to be, we must encourage the function of spiritual gifts; they create an expectancy in the hearts of the people that God will respond to them and speak specifically to their questions and needs.

The Church in the city must be a worshiping Church. Celebration is a vital witness to the world, and it also enables the people to be refreshed spiritually in the presence of the Lord.

Joy is a vital ingredient of the life of the Church in the city. To quench this joy through heavy-handed leadership and staid worship styles not only discourages urban church growth, but stunts the maturing of God's people.

6. *The power of a missionary vision.*

It is obvious that the church in Antioch was concerned about others. This is seen in their involvement with the poor (Acts 11:29), and their willingness to send out their top leadership in missionary endeavors.

The test of any church's commitment to missions is its willingness to send its very best to help in the missionary enterprise. Far too many urban churches become overwhelmed with the needs around them and lose a broader vision. A church that becomes ingrown and insular will discourage big-hearted people with potential for Christian service from attending the church. They will soon learn that there is a grasping, controlling spirit rather than a generous spirit among the leaders. They will discover that the church leadership is not committed to building up their gifts and sending them out, but rather keeping them there to build up the local church program.

One pastor I know believes he is to discourage all interest in missions on the part of individual lay people in the congregation. His philosophy is that if God wants them to go, they will overcome his wet blanket approach and make it somehow. The lack of Christlikeness and generosity in this attitude has discouraged many in his congregation from following Christ in Christian service. Though this church has been blessed by God, I have often wondered how much more blessing it would have experienced had the pastor had a more Christlike approach to the longings of some of his parishioners to reach out to others.

The pastor and ministry team who decide to equip God's people for service will reap the reward of seeing those they serve extend the outreach of the Church throughout the world.

7. *The power of Christlikeness.*

In Antioch the believers were first called Christians. Something about their lives warranted a response from the non-Christian community. In that center of idolatry and commercial competition, the Christians made such an impact on the city that they had to be recognized.

The power of the witness of the church in Antioch is an encouragement that we, too, can make an impact on the cities of our world. To have this influence we must follow our Lord Jesus.

Paul and Philippi

It is difficult to select one city that represents the amazing contribution the apostle Paul made to the expansion of the Church in the first century. Paul was an urban apostle. Athens, Rome, Corinth, Jerusalem, Antioch, Ephesus and many other cities felt the impact of the ministry of this great man. But one city's significance outshines them all, and that was the first city to receive the Gospel in Europe. The Holy Spirit had forbidden Paul and his team to go into Asia, and instead gave a compelling vision that they were to preach the Gospel in Macedonia. Ten miles along from the tiny port city of Neapolis lay the ancient city of Philippi. It was named in honor of Philip II of Macedon, the one-eyed father of Alexander the Great.

In 334 B.C., using Philippi as one of his major European bases, Alexander the Great invaded Asia. Now, in stark contrast, Paul was using Asia as his base to invade Europe with the Gospel. Paul's tiny missionary band comprised Silas (often called Silvanus), Timothy (who joined him in Lystra and whom Paul often referred to as his beloved son) and Luke (the Gentile physician who joined with Paul at Troas). Determined that the Gospel be proclaimed in Europe, God arrested Paul's attention by a dramatic vision in the night while he was in the city of Troas. In what today we might call a charismatic experience, Paul was brought up short by the living God, and no doubt began to ponder deeply the implication of crossing over into the continent of Europe.

As Paul sailed into Neapolis, and then trudged the ten-mile journey up to Philippi, he was no doubt aware of the history of this great city. It was here that Brutus and Cassius—assassins of Julius Caesar—clashed with the armies of Octavian and Anthony. Being a citizen of Tarsus, Paul had a distinct reason to recall the importance of that great battle.

Following Caesar's assassination, Cassius took flight with his brother-in-law Brutus from Rome. Cassius eventually ended up in Tarsus, ordered his soldiers to live in the homes of the wealthy and, in the words of Ludwig, "coldly announced that he wouldn't leave until he was paid nine million dollars." To raise that fantastic sum, public lands were auctioned, silver and gold vessels from the temples were melted and the free were sold into slavery. First to be enslaved were boys, then girls, then men and women, and finally old people. Many killed themselves rather than submit. Though this had happened almost two hundred years before the time of Paul, every citizen in Tarsus knew the terrible things done there by Cassius.

Thus when Paul of Tarsus entered the city of Philippi, he must have wondered how God was going to lead him to penetrate this city. His normal pattern was to go to a synagogue and preach. Finding no synagogue in the city of Philippi, Paul was forced to adopt new and creative methods. He heard that there was a place of prayer by the riverside where a number of women gathered to worship each Sabbath. It is fascinating to note that Paul did not hesitate to proclaim the Gospel to an audience solely of women. And it is even more fascinating to note that the first church to be planted on the continent of Europe was made up of female converts and led initially by a woman. Lydia compelled Paul and his team to receive hospitality with her (Acts 16:15), and it was in her home that the church in Philippi gathered for worship and instruction.

Not only is this church significant because it illustrates Paul's often-disputed openness to women in general, and specifically to women in leadership; it also demonstrates the power of a church with a missionary vision. Writing to the Philippian church ten years later, in A.D. 60, Paul thanked the Philippians for their partnership in mission "from the first day until now" (Philippians 1:4–5; 4:15–16).

Dr. Bill Lane stresses the need to appreciate the extent of the Philippians' partnership with Paul. He points out that their missionary ministry was extended through Paul, their adopted missionary, to Thessalonica, which in turn spread the Gospel throughout Asia. They also supported Paul and prayed for him while he was in Corinth. This enabled him to devote his full attention to the ministry of preaching the Gospel while in that city.

When there was a famine in Judea, God placed a burden on Paul's heart to bring a gift to the Christians in Jerusalem. Paul talked about the participation of the Philippians in that ministry of mercy as well (2 Corinthians 8:1–5).

Paul also thanked the Philippians for their involvement with him in the city of Rome (Philippians 2:25; 4:18). The Philippian letter was primarily a thank-you letter to the church, after they had sent a gift to Paul while he was under house arrest in the city of Rome. Going further than sending their finances, they sent a gifted member of the congregation, Epaphroditus, to work with Paul in the training of believers in the imperial city.

When you think of one congregation impacting such cities as Thessalonica, Corinth, Jerusalem and Rome, you begin to understand the breadth of the vision of this church. Its commitment to missions, its willingness to adopt a missionary not from its own church, and the breadth and extent of its vision are all examples to churches today. This was no selfish congregation with a limited Kingdom perspective. These people were willing to stand with Paul through thick and thin. They sent their money and their best people. They participated with him in relief and development, church planting, evangelism, education and training.

Dr. Lane points out that 75 years after Paul wrote his letter to the Philippians, Polycarp—the senior pastor of the church in Smyrna—wrote these words to the Philippians:

> I have greatly rejoiced with you in our Lord Jesus Christ
> . . . because the strong root of your faith, which was

spoken of in days long past, endures even until now and brings forth fruit to our Lord Jesus Christ (First Letter of Polycarp to the Philippians).

*　　*　　*

These four men and these four cities offer a variety of models for the Church today in her presence in the urban world. The Church in the city is called to a complex task. Though the message and the methods we use are simple, we must understand the complexities around us. To those who are called to the proclamation of the Gospel, appreciation for the role of the prophet is essential. For those who work diligently and silently behind the scenes in community development, cooperation with church planters and evangelists is vital. The Church of Jesus Christ must develop an integrated approach to the complex urban world in which we live. Doing so will enhance the message of the Gospel and increase the impact we have on the lives of men and women in the city.

8
Searching for the Urban Nomad

He is wiry, feet toughened from much walking. A simple robe thrown over his shoulder, a staff in hand to pace the journey.

With his few possessions packed and loaded onto the backs of his livestock, his eyes are on the horizon, where home will be tomorrow.

He is the rural nomad, instantly recognizable as he trails his livelihood to fresh pastureland—poor and rootless, but through Western eyes viewed with a sense of romanticism; a part of vanishing history, the lost tradition of centuries.

Recent years, marked by the explosive growth of the world's cities, have seen the emergence of this nomadic countryman's metropolitan cousins—those whom I and others who have ministered in cities for the past few years have come to identify as urban nomads. But with crowded streets replacing wide open spaces, urban nomads are not so easily spotted.

They may be the ones in the Nike running shoes. Or power-dressed in sharp suits with leather attaché cases. Perhaps ragged jeans and a pocketful of marijuana. Even turbans and supermarket shopping bags.

They can be students, unskilled workers, upwardly mobile professionals, artists and musicians, drug addicts, prostitutes, criminals, tourists, the mentally ill and the homeless.

They move into town to seek new work, escape old problems, stay a few months or even a couple of years and then up and move on. It could be that they are trying to keep one step ahead of the law, or not get left behind in the chase to make more money.

Some even settle down and stay longer, but the chances are that you wouldn't recognize them if they lived on your own street, and they share with their more restless relatives the same essential characteristic that makes them urban nomads.

They may live, work and play in the city, but their real "home" is somewhere else. As such they fail to put down any real roots, never really identify with the community at large and people beyond their own small group of contacts.

And that can make them perhaps invisible to most Christians, and often seemingly unreachable for the rest.

But they are there. The thousands of homeless across the United States, trailing from one city to the next. The mine workers of Soweto, leaving their homelands to find work to support their families. Then there are the six million-plus street children of Brazil, without parents or a permanent roof over their heads.

In India there are the Bhojpuri Bihari's of Calcutta, forced to leave their farmlands through drought, famine and crop failure. Now they work as rickshaw porters or taxi drivers, often living in the open near railway stations or in small slums.

Tibetans come down from the mountains each winter to New Delhi and Katmandhu, where they make their income from their handwoven clothes before returning home in the summer months. According to missionaries I know working in these parts they are among the hardest groups to reach, still untouched by the Gospel and, like so many of their fellow urban nomads, just skimming the surface of the towns and cities.

Bringing Jesus to the urban nomads of our world is one of the great challenges facing the Church in the complex, confusing task of seeing the Gospel proclaimed and demonstrated in the cities.

During my travels and talks with those working in cities on every continent, I have come to see that for all the outward differences, there are really two distinct types of urban nomad.

There are those who have been *pushed* to the city, and those who have been *pulled*. Generally speaking, many of those who have been pushed are in third-world cities.

They are there because of outside forces that have propelled them from their rural homelands—drought, famine, unemployment, fighting and tribal conflicts, each acting as a route sign to the nearest city.

They may move as families, swelling the shantytowns and favellas that spread around the edges of countless big cities, but still connected in heart with the land and other people they have had to leave behind.

Many times, too, they arrive alone, the father or husband seeking work so that he can send money home. Older children, too, looking to earn enough to send home to support the rest of the family.

Perhaps a couple of times a year they will be able to make the journey back to see their loved ones. The rest of the time they are too busy working long hours to think about making their new surroundings home, even if they wanted to.

Then there are those—usually but not exclusively—in the Western nations who have been pulled to the cities. They are there not so much because of what they can leave behind, but for what they can find.

The lure of education, career success, easy money, plenty of work, fast friendships, drugs, sex and prestige all draw to the big cities. They often arrive alone, with the network of familiar friends and family left behind.

It is estimated that around twenty percent of all urban dwellers move *each year*. The resulting breakdown in extended family ties, and the problems that can cause in the nuclear home, are well documented . . . and all too obvious.

Not all these Westernized urban nomads are part of what might be called mainstream life, of course. Some are the "marginalized" people of society. They have either dropped out, fallen out or been thrown out. They could be rebels or seekers, crime and abuse victims, the criminals and the mentally ill.

But the majority of these Western-style urban nomads would not stand out in a line at the local supermarket, bank or cinema.

Reaching these urban nomads with the Gospel is not an easy task. But it is essential that we try for two reasons. The first is that they are, obviously, part of the "whole world" of

Jesus' Great Commission. They have as much right and need to hear as anyone.

The second is that they can also be a doorway into some of the more remote parts of the world currently beyond our reach. Wars and famines may have different causes, but God is using these and other situations to urbanize the world.

It is no longer necessary to go to North Africa to reach the Algerians, for example. Today fourteen percent of the world's Algerian population can be found in Paris. That is a trend repeated in countless cultural and language groups.

So in reaching the urban nomads of our cities, we can plant seeds that will be carried back into their distant homes, families and networks. And while there is a downside to the characteristics of the urban nomad, there is also a potential great strength.

In many cases, urban nomads are used to living simply. Either they are struggling to make ends meet themselves, or they are supporting extended families elsewhere, so they are not preoccupied with making themselves settled and comfortable where they are.

Their transient lifestyle means they are likely to be more ready to follow Jesus wherever He may lead them, carrying the Gospel perhaps across national boundaries, languages and cultures.

Nor are they so attached to permanence and physical relationships that they would be held back from leaving, if the Lord should tell them it was time to move on. Indeed, deep in them, somewhere, is the essence of pilgrimage—the biblical truth that here is not our home, we are only passing through.

Herein is one of the difficulties of reaching them in the first place, of course. The nomadic lifestyle also tends to militate against the sense of community and committedness that is at the heart of the Gospel. Having said that, I realize it is often because they have been alienated by their past experiences. The addicts and prostitutes of our cities are sinners, yes, but oftentimes they are the sinned against, too.

So we will not reach the urban nomads, I believe, by door-to-door visitation and arranging big evangelistic rallies. City-wide strategies are not going to work. We need to start by thinking small.

We need to identify one of the "streams" of nomads, and look to see how we might make contact.

It could be students or members of an ethnic community; they may be second- or third-generation in the city, but they are still urban nomads because their whole culture and sense of identity keep them rooted elsewhere. They may wake up each morning in your city, but they go to sleep each night in another part of the world.

Where do we start? By seeking to identify with that grouping—geographically or socially. It may mean changing your leisure patterns to bring you into contact.

And once there, it means compassion and commitment. Compassion that wants to identify with their hurts and needs instead of throwing out a too-hasty Gospel challenge; that looks to listen and understand the questions before offering a glib answer.

Determining to stay, giving the time necessary to build the trust and acceptance that can lead to relationships, and then the long haul of living out God's redemptive love as part of a whole-life witness. Inviting them into our homes, becoming their friends.

With Calcutta's Bhojpuri Bihari, for example, the doorway might be in helping them provide for their families. It need not mean a huge investment, either—perhaps a church raising enough money to buy a dozen or so rickshaws, license them and then rent them out. Each day the porter would repay a small portion of his earnings, until over a period of time he had repaid the loan, and owned his own rickshaw.

Not only would such a scheme see the Gospel "talked" in practical language; it would also begin to establish a reputation of trust with the Bihari—an important ingredient in a city where Christianity is often not viewed with great sympathy.

And as such a small, church-sized plan illustrates, it is not those in full-time Christian ministries who, alone, are the ones to tackle this issue. It is a challenge to the whole Church, and perhaps best responded to by the local church.

It means taking a new look at our cities and trying to understand them from God's perspective. After fifteen years helping to pioneer urban ministries, I am convinced that a city is not so much a place as a process—less of a melting pot, where values and cultures all get stirred into one common flavor, than a salad bowl in which they are tossed together in a randomly creative kind of way.

I believe that to turn our backs on the city is to turn away from God's eternal purposes of salvation and justice for His whole creation.

Reaching the urban nomads with the good news of the Kingdom of Jesus Christ—Someone who, incidentally, also lived a transient life—will involve not just seeing change brought to their lifestyle and understanding . . . but ours, too.

9
A Strategy for Reaching Cities

Though the word *strategy* seems impersonal and uncaring, it is important for us to ask how a concerned church or individual should approach a city. What strategy or means should be employed in order to make the maximum impact for Christ? The city is so large, contains so many people, has so many needs. . . . Where do we start?

There will no doubt be as many approaches to urban mission as there are concerned Christians. This is helpful, particularly if the energy and effort of believers are guided by a biblical vision. The Bible does not hold us to one particular approach to ministry methodology. The Scriptures unfold a variety of approaches and ministries used by God to have an impact on cities.

Still, there are certain common elements to biblical urban mission that every individual, ministry team, family and church hoping to serve Christ effectively in the city should know. There is, moreover, a unifying framework that all be-lievers in the city are a part of. This chapter will examine four stages of urban mission that make up this framework and some of the basic elements of each stage.

It should be noted that I am not suggesting formulas that guarantee success, however that is defined. I am saying that all Christians in the city, no matter what their theological perspective, educational achievement or level of maturity, are members of the whole Church in the whole city. Awareness of God's purposes for His Church in the city increases our ap-preciation of others—our unity—and our comprehension of God—our faith.

There is an attitude toward ministry and residence in the city that one could call an "entrance strategy" to urban mis-sion, something that is pre-mission in nature. Some of this has been touched on already: genuine love for people, faith in God in spite of great need, giving up our rights.

One more aspect warrants mentioning here, and that is teachableness. If we come to the city as learners, rather than evangelists, social workers, families on a mission for God, churches that care, or whatever else we dream up as our rea-son to be in the city, we will be protected from making a million mistakes and we will be far more Christlike in the process.

Living in the city is a learning process. We will learn about cultures, people, life, pain, ourselves, failure, and if we learn all these lessons, along the way we will learn to be God's answer to others.

Let's use the apostle Paul as a model for urban strategy. His life more than any other demonstrates an integrated approach to urban mission and evangelism. This is not meant to detract from the life of Christ, for in a unique way Paul was commissioned by the Lord Jesus to pioneer the presence of the Church in the cities of that day.

Conversion of Sinners

In his very helpful book *Apostles to the City*, Roger Greenway points out that Paul's strategy in cities had a definite pattern:

> The lines of Paul's urban strategy ran from converts, to churches, to the whole Roman society—its governments, institutions and religions. Paul moved out into the highly urbanized Roman world of his day with a definite strategy in mind.
> (p. 81)

Paul targeted cities consciously. He focused on the major urban centers of his day. Philippi was a major administrative center and was situated on an important trade route. Thessalonica was a strategic port for the Roman navy, located on the Ignatian Way. Corinth was provincial capital for Achaia, a port, banking center and home of the Ismian games. The list goes on: Athens, Rome, Ephesus, Jerusalem.

In these cities Paul believed God for converts. No matter the political, social or spiritual state of affairs, he preached the Gospel. His missionary strategy was built on the bedrock of personal conversion. He stood counter to Roman emperor worship and Hellenistic syncretism; he declared that Jesus was the Christ, the long-awaited Messiah and Savior of all mankind.

The heart of authentic urban strategy is bringing people to Christ. This is the touchstone for all we do in the city.

Whether we are involved with the poor or the rich, the powerless or the powerful, our presence should be motivated by the desire to see people lay down their reasons for rejecting Christ and embrace Him as their Lord and Savior.

We are not speaking of easy-believism. The city does not need a lightweight, superficial gospel that promises everything for nothing. Sinners are rebels. No matter what their class in society, each man and woman has personally ratified Adam's rebellion against God and needs to be confronted with Christ's claim of Lordship on their lives. The rich man must surrender his wealth and the poor man his bitterness; each person will stand before God to give an account of his life.

Care for the Poor

The agonizing question of whether we should preach the Gospel or care for the poor is not a biblical one. There is no dichotomy in the Scriptures between caring and preaching. People are created in God's image, body and soul; we are to do both.

Evangelists should not proclaim the Gospel among the poor unless there is someone to follow through and provide a practical expression of the love of Christ. They have a responsibility to identify with a caring community of believers so that their proclamation is seen as part of Christ's concern for their needs.

And the ones caring for the poor must never do so without declaring that their care is given in the name of Christ. Christian organizations cannot accept government offers to serve in a nation without the freedom to do so in Jesus' name.

The apostle Paul demonstrated his concern for the poor, to

the point of turning away from his desire to go to Spain and "fully [preach] the gospel of Christ, thus making it my ambition to preach the gospel, not where Christ has already been named" (Romans 15:19–20). Instead, Paul persevered in his commitment to those suffering from famine in Jerusalem, in spite of repeated warnings that he would be imprisoned if he returned to that city.

Church Planting Among the Unreached

Church planting is essential urban strategy. Paul was not satisfied with bringing individuals to Christ. He was concerned with winning sheep *and* building flocks. He gathered believers together wherever he preached, and organizing churches was central to his entire approach in the city.

Paul was assigned the task of planting churches as an apostle and pioneer of the faith. His zeal in doing it was based on his revelation of the importance of the Body of Christ. As Roger Greenway explains:

> By revelation he had come to understand that the church was the long-awaited messianic community, the bearer of the gospel to all races and nations. It was through the church that God would now fulfill his redemptive purpose for the world. (p. 8)

That insight made Paul a church planter. He believed that God in Christ was carrying out His long-awaited redemptive work in the world through the Church.

We need the same revelation as Paul. Not only is the Church the covenant community of God's people on earth; it is the only way traumatized masses of urban poor will find healing for their broken lives. Through joyful, worshiping, caring communities they have hope. The Church is one of God's primary ways of channeling love and hope to His people.

Christ's Lordship Over Society

Paul planted the seeds in his preaching and teaching that would eventually lead the early Church to proclaim Christ's Lordship over every aspect of society. His vision of the Kingdom touched all dimensions of life. He addressed the role of government (Romans 13), the relationship of slaves to their masters (Philemon, Ephesians 5), the nature and function of the family (Ephesians 5) and the responsibilities of the rich to the poor (1 Timothy 6). There is a refreshing breadth to Paul's teaching that is often missed by the Church today. Though he was a church planter and evangelist, his comprehensive view of the Lordship of Christ was far more extensive than many realize.

Because he did not challenge the institution of slavery head-on, that does not mean he did not address the necessity of its demise. And because he did not write one of his epistles specifically on the subject of injustice, that does not mean Paul was silent on the economic and political issues of his day (see 1 Timothy 6:2; 2 Thessalonians 3:6–12; Titus 3:1).

Paul not only instilled in his converts a love for the lost; he also taught and encouraged them to take up their responsibilities as contributing members of the cities and nations they inhabited. He also challenged the idols of his day. The riots in Ephesus that resulted from Paul's prophetic preaching let the churches know that political and economic issues were their concern.

If churches and missionaries fail to understand that Jesus intends His Lordship to be over all of life, they will not be able to disciple the future leaders of the cities they are reaching with the Gospel. It is natural for an evangelist to want all his converts to be evangelists as well. But some are called to be bankers, lawyers, educators, government officials and spokesmen in the media.

The churches Paul planted were the leaven of society. They were models of righteousness. Paul knew that the men and women he won to Christ were to be formed into congregations, and then sent into the world as salt and light. Some were to be missionaries to the unreached. Others were to be God's agents in the marketplace or the military. Instructed in God's ways, they became aware of the issues they faced and the great difference between their faith and the idolatries around them. To quote Greenway, "Gradually the false gods of Rome were identified, the battle joined, and the idols began to fall" (p. 86).

Bible-believing Christians, particularly Christians who are city-dwellers, must perceive the issues of righteousness and justice, know where to draw the battle lines and engage the demonic urban idols challenging Christ's rulership over every aspect of city life.

A Declaration of War

In every stage of urban mission, believers should be closely related to a local church, ministering in close-knit teams and acquainted with the power of the Holy Spirit (Romans 15:19).

Urban mission is warfare. To proclaim Christ's Kingdom is to challenge Satan's kingdom. Urban idols are demonic in nature, and when believers appear on the scene we threaten the domination that powers and principalities have had.

The presence of the Church in the city is a sign to the powers that their hold on people is at an end. The Church is a sign of God's redeeming grace. Our presence in a neighborhood is a living symbol of Christ's power to conquer any bondage. No wonder the demons make such a fuss when the Church moves in. But to those who understand the spirits of the city and the urban mission of the Church, it is confirmation of Christ's victory.

Part 4
Families in the City

10
Parenthood in Peril

"The family" no longer exists in the Western world. In its place are many families, of diverse styles and shapes. There are single-parent families, stepfamilies, gay families and non-marital families. We are living through a period of historic change in the structure and function of the family.

The upheaval is evident everywhere in our culture. To quote one news magazine, "Babies have babies . . . kids refuse to grow up and leave home, affluent yuppies prize their BMW's more than their children, rich and poor children alike blow their minds with drugs, people casually move in with each other and out again."

Human society is increasingly dominated by urban life, and this has particularly affected the family. The century of industrial development from the 1830s to the 1930s saw a marked increase in urban population. In the United States 73 percent of the population is urbanized.

Poor housing, vandalism, poverty and many other factors have contributed to the disintegration of the family in our nation's cities. While the government's approach has been woefully inadequate, amounting to little more than first-aid treatment for areas of acute need, the Church has not done much better. Its response to the breakup of the family and the pressures it faces is sadly lacking in relevance and urgency.

The divorce rate for families in the United States has doubled since 1965, and sociologists predict that half of all first marriages will end in divorce. Six out of ten second marriages will collapse. One-third of all the children born in our nation will most likely live in a stepfamily before they are eighteen years of age.

Children are paying the price for their parents' confusion. Two-thirds of all mothers and more than half of all mothers of infants are in the work force. Divorce has left a devastated generation in its wake, and for many children the pain is compounded by confusion due to materialistic indulgence, neglect, lack of discipline and sometimes abject poverty. It is estimated that more than seventy percent of all violent-impulse crimes in the United States are committed by the children of single-parent families.

Western Christians are fearful for the family in the future. They are just beginning to face the reality that exchanging old-fashioned family values for financial independence and a comfortable lifestyle is exacting a very high price. People are beginning to face up to the reality that husbands, wives and children are not getting enough out of family life. People are hurting. The family in Western society has become dysfunctional.

The biblical definition of a family is that a man and woman

love each other and are committed to each other through marriage, and that they raise children in an atmosphere of trust, commitment and loving discipline. By contrast the American Census Bureau has settled on another definition of the family: "Two or more persons related by birth, marriage or adoption who reside in the same household." New York State's highest court stretched this definition recently, and held that the survivor of a gay couple retained the legal right to an apartment they had long shared, just as a surviving husband or wife would.

But to call homosexual households "families" is ridiculous. One social critic says, "You can't fool mother nature. The family is a mommy and a daddy and their children."

Most Christians are yet to take seriously the effects of the Industrial Revolution on the family. The family was once a close-knit unit of production, held together by the need to support one another. The modern family is now a unit of consumption. The old values of work, savings and family togetherness have been replaced by ideals of financial independence and rapid affluence. The modern family is driven by the twin goals of prosperity and independence. Wealth and comfort are now seen as rights rather than the results of hard work.

The Industrial Revolution also led to vast changes in *how* we live. The family that was once held together by work is now pulled apart by television and the car.

Figures from annual Census reports reveal that fewer than 27 percent of the United States' 91 million households in 1988 fit the traditional model of the family.

Unfortunately, these trends are not limited to the American or British scene. Nearly half of all children born in Denmark,

Iceland and Sweden are born out of wedlock. Shunning the word *illegitimate*, demographers now refer to children born out of wedlock as "non-marital children."

Four out of seven marriages in Sweden fail—one of the highest divorce rates in the Western world. In the twenty to thirty age group half of Sweden's couples who live together are unmarried.

Legislators in Sweden have granted unmarried partners living together a legal status equal with married couples. Tax questions, rental agreements, insurance issues and other judicial matters lead increasingly to calls to confer equal status— whether it involves heterosexual or homosexual partners. According to *World Christian News*, Denmark became the first country to legalize homosexual unions in October 1989. Although the "registered partnerships" are not called marriages, their legal ramifications approximate heterosexual matrimony.

Youthhood

Sociologist Kenneth Woodward declares, "The age of extended adolescence has arrived." Adolescence is a time of intense self-absorption and learning—a time when young people find out who they are and what their philosophy of life is.

Adulthood, on the other hand, is a time to develop character and the other qualities of life that are essential to live as a mature member of society. Such character traits as initiative, competence, commitment, determination, honesty and integrity are all part of this growing-up process.

By these standards, young people entering the twenty-first century are far less mature than their ancestors. The generation of baby boomer kids—those born between 1946 and

1964—is maturing earlier than previous generations, but emotionally they are taking longer to make adult choices.

"Youthhood" is the extended period of life between adolescence and adulthood. Christian leaders mourn the loss of mature teenagers. In generations past youth could be counted on to be reliable emotionally. The present generation is a product of an extremely affluent society and is not willing to pay the price to enter the world of hard realities. Many come from dysfunctional families.

By the time they reach eighteen years of age 57 percent of American teenagers have had sex. This is the generation of the one-night stand. More than two-thirds of all abortions are performed on single women under the age of 27. Some young women have multiple abortions. The ease with which these young people choose to abort reflects a disturbing sense of self-absorption and an alarming indifference to the moral gravity of their actions.

This is the generation that is committed not to be committed. Half of all thirty-year-olds cohabit before marriage. Many are of the assumption that marriage won't work for the long haul. Studies now demonstrate that couples who cohabit before marriage are more likely to divorce than those who do not.

The influence of television, with its ability to provide instant, incessant and intellectually passive diversion, is a major cause of protracted immaturity. The endless hours of watching the tube and listening to pop music has bred a passive population of young people. The evidence of this passivity can be found in the changing vision that students have of life after college. One sociologist points out that in the early '70s the most cherished value for university students was developing a meaningful philosophy of life. By the end of the '80s that value had dropped to ninth, far behind the first choice of "being well-off financially."

The baby boomers were brought up in the most affluent society in human history, yet they display an undercurrent of dissatisfaction, a feeling that something has gone very wrong with their world. The boomers have become the yuppies, and they have learned that even two-income families cannot buy happiness.

Minority Families

On the other side of the city—economically and physically—live urban blacks. Harvie Conn, editor of *Urban Mission*, says,

> Of all Americans, they appear to be most vulnerable to current trends of family disillusion. As long ago as 1982 almost 30% of all black families were female-headed households with children, in contrast to 7% of white families.

Breakup of the black family lends itself to racist stereotypes. Many whites assume that blacks are "immoral, irresponsible and incapable of keeping their families together." Some people call this the syndrome of "blaming the victim." The sickness of the black family is assumed to be the cause of the deterioration of the black community, rather than the symptom.

Black pastor Wellington Boone asserts that the welfare system led to the breakup of the black family. "Slavery decimated the black family. But for the next hundred years blacks began to rebuild the traditional family values brought with them from Africa. Then liberals with their vision of a great society began to hand out money to solve problems that they were not willing to get involved with on a personal basis." Boone and many other blacks believe that the welfare system contributed to the breakup of the family, encouraging black fathers not to marry and mothers to have more children so that the per-child allowance would continue.

At the same time, urban black families draw on coping devices. Neighbors develop a close community to help raise children. The black extended family reaches past bloodlines and turns next-door neighbors into "uncles" and "aunts." black men have developed a "soul brother" relationship.

By the year 2000, forty million Hispanics will live in the United States. We have much to learn from traditional Hispanic family life. The strong bonds of family commitment in the Hispanic culture are a model to study closely. Though the strength of the family is now being challenged by gangs and drugs, much can be learned from them about what the post-suburban Western world should look like. This is in spite of the fact that economic pressures have forced many Hispanic men to leave their families in Mexico and Central America. At present one-third of all Hispanic children live in single-parent homes in the United States.

Families in Need

The most basic unit in society, even more basic than the Church, is the family. In the opening pages of the Bible God describes His intent for a man and woman to cleave together and raise children in an atmosphere of godly love and purity. The salvation of the family lies not only in the proclamation of the Gospel, but in Christian families themselves finding new meaning and purpose by a commitment to Christian service. In order for the Christian family to find focus it must be a family that commits itself to sacrificial service to others. The opportunities are there for those who want to get involved.

11
Families with a Mission

To the Editor
Christianity Today
Wheaton, Illinois,
USA

Dear Sir,

I just read an article in *Christianity Today* entitled "Growing Up a World Away" (February '89). I felt that there was something I really wanted to share about this article.

I am an MK [missionaries' kid]. My parents were missionaries in a central Asian country where I was born, and I now live in the Netherlands where I have grown up. I found your article fascinating but there was something I felt was missing.

My parents have always *included* us in our choices on "the mission field." They have encouraged us to pray and ask God for His guidance, personally, for all the decisions we make.

161

I would like to suggest when God calls "Mom and Dad" to be missionaries He is not forgetting their children! I have asked for, and received, a very personal calling and burden for the country we live in. God has called me too! And if God has called me, no blame can rest on my parents. We were encouraged to pray about what kind of schooling we should have and as a result my brother and I have chosen two different schools (he attended an international school, I attended a Dutch public school). So any adjustment I might have to make, or extra schooling I'll have to do, if I feel God is wanting me to attend college in the States, is just that—an adjustment I'll have to make. It is not a major problem. I believe it might even be part of God's overall plan for my life.

Problems/questions should not be missionaries' children and their schooling—the question should be: Have I asked God what *He* wants? And I really missed hearing that in your article. God created the family and He doesn't just call half of it, He calls it as a whole. Kids need to be encouraged to grasp and accept that calling for themselves personally. Any resentment a kid might feel is probably because he is dragged along and not included in those decisions that so majorly affect his life, too! God knows what is best for us.

Why not ask Him?! (And ask Him *with* your children!)

Sincerely,
Misha McClung (16)

Growing Up in a City

Growing up in a city, just like growing up on the mission field, has a certain amount of glory and a certain amount of pain.

Misha's letter reflects some of the glory. When you raise kids—whether in an American city or in another nation—and include them in the decisions that affect their lives, they grow up with an excitement about hearing God's voice for themselves.

Raising kids in a city, just like on a mission field, has its disadvantages. Sometimes they are not able to play outside with the other kids; it is too rough or dangerous. Often there is noplace to play. But the glory of living in the city far outweighs the pain. In fact, the pain becomes glorious when we look at it in the right way. The glory of God is often found in the most difficult circumstances. Who would have thought that God would have sent *His* Son to suffer the humiliating, cruel and painful death of the cross? But in that horrendous moment, the magnificence of God's goodness and glory is fully manifested.

The glory of raising kids in the city has to do with the magnificence of God's Spirit fleshed out in our lives in the neighborhoods where we live. The glory of God is the triumph of His grace meeting people's needs in real-life situations. The glory is seeing our children get involved in other people's lives and learn to rely on God's Spirit in those situations.

In the early years of our ministry, I saw too much glory in my "ministry" and it caused me to spend too much time away from home. I actually missed some of the glory of our home as I immersed myself in hours of counseling and street evangelism. Fortunately, my dear wife, Sally, would not let me escape into my own little world of glory; the faithful reminder of her needs and those of our two children rescued me from my own inglorious fate.

Today, having lived in Amsterdam since 1971, the glory far outshines the pain. Our kids have grown, and have turned out beautifully. This city has definitely helped shape them into the vibrant, concerned, thoughtful, international kids they are. To quote one Christian leader, "If we could do it all over again, we would do it all over again."

Through the years of living in Christian community, my very practical wife, two very honest children and I have learned lessons about what we would do differently if there were a next time. The question of families raising kids in the city is complex and multifaceted. No family situation is the same as another. No two cities are the same, no two suburbs are the same, no two families are the same and no two perceptions are the same.

The Pain

It is important to face honestly the disadvantages of raising kids in the city.

The Pain of Mistrust

The pain of racial separation exists in the city. White kids are often a minority and they feel like it. This separation affects the children's playtime. They cannot talk to strangers, they cannot play in the park, they cannot go outside after dark, they never open the door when their parents are gone, they don't leave a bicycle outside (or it's gone) and they have to be very careful to pay attention to what is going on around them.

White parents who live in Asian, black or Hispanic neighborhoods must also face the pain of separation. There may be mistrust. Ethnic minorities look with suspicion upon whites who move into their neighborhoods. White do-gooders are not wanted, although genuine friends are.

The Pain of Time Limits

Parents who live in challenging neighborhoods have the constant opportunity to care not only for their own children but for the children of others as well. Because they are surrounded by families and children in need there is a tremendous pull on them to be involved with lots of house guests. Busy moms and dads are also pulled into church gatherings, community meetings and responses to late-night emergencies.

The Pain of Physical Danger

Walking down the street and being confronted with a knife or getting knocked off your bicycle is not a lot of fun. Being a woman and always fearing a physical attack is not an easy pressure to live with.

The Pain of Sensory Overload

Children and parents learn to live with continual input to the eyes, ears and nose. There are rancid smells—walls on which people have urinated. The sound of traffic and street conversation is ever-present. Some cultures find this sensory input a painful process, but for others it is the very essence of life. The busyness, the close contact, the sights and the sounds of the city create a sense of security and well-being for many cultures.

The Pain of Lost Association

If the city your family chooses to live in is located in another country or is different in other respects from the place in which you parents were reared, you will undoubtedly miss having your children experience your own childhood associations. It was quite different for me when we took our children back to the States and they did not know the Pledge of Allegiance to the flag, something every American schoolchild learns.

Sally was shocked when she tried to explain to our son, Matthew, how important the Alamo is in the history of Texas, her home state. To her attempts at a spontaneous history lesson about the great Republic of Texas Matthew quipped, "Isn't the Alamo a rent-a-car agency?" Sally's face revealed her disappointment that her son did not share the deep feelings she had about the words *Remember the Alamo*.

The Glory

When God's character is fleshed out in real-life family situations, the consequence is principles learned. Those principles work in every culture. Before we look at the principles and how to apply them, let us first look at some of the reasons urban life can be so glorious. The following quotes are from Matthew about why he enjoys urban life:

- Something that I like about the city is that it doesn't lack in excitement—there is always something to do and it's not real boring.
- In this city in particular, transportation is good; you don't always have to rely on cars to take you around.
- This city has a nice atmosphere. I know there are some thieves and criminals and so on, but the majority of the population are not like that and there is just a sense of a lot of people being together in one place. That's nice.
- The city is like a two-faced place. There are nice people

and there are unkind people. You have to watch your back now and then so that you don't get robbed or mugged or anything, but you can meet people here; you can have friendships.

• There is no lack of activity. There are plenty of things to do, such as playing billiards or going swimming, going for a walk in the park, going to a movie, going out for dinner. There are lots of different types of restaurants here from all different countries in the world. Shopping is also very convenient.

• There are lots of different cultures here. You can meet lots of really interesting people—people from all over the world, such as people from Africa, South America, the Caribbean, Asia.

• There are lots of different parades. We see the Dutch Santa Claus come in every year. There are lots of protests, demonstrations, all sorts of different things that we get to see here that you don't have in little tiny towns.

No Pain—No Gain

As a parent I have tried conscientiously to reflect over the benefits versus the disadvantages for my children in raising them in the city. One wonderful benefit is cross-cultural sensitivity. Children learn what it is like to be discriminated against. They also learn to see people as real people and not as stereotypes or caricatures. They see and taste foods from all over the world. They experience people struggling with pressures and opportunities that in their own culture they would never experience. They see lonely children on the streets. The effects of alcohol, drugs and promiscuous sex are ever present before their eyes. Shelter them from this? No way. I hope it affects them to the point that they want to get involved. I pray God will use it to shape their values and ambitions in life.

Another benefit of urban life comes when children learn that everything in life is a gift from God and that those of us who have a secure home and an intact family are immensely blessed. Our children have learned to live in two worlds, the world of their home culture and the world of their adopted culture. They learn that they are indeed pilgrims on this earth.

Urban children are raised in a spiritual environment that is forged out of necessity. To be living as strangers in a neighborhood among people from different nationalities is a tremendous challenge to the prayer life and the commitment of a family. Children can have a vision instilled in them for ministry and for the world that will never come by living in cultural and ethnic insularity.

Children learn about the fallen nature of man in a city. The city contains both the best and the worst of human nature and human civilization. Crime *is* in the city. Children see before them the fallen nature of man and have the opportunity to respond on a daily basis.

To quote the son of one urban pastor, Paul Van der Klay, in *Urban Mission*:

> Children learn that by moving to the city they are not going to be there primarily to help fend for the poor and the sick and the needy; what they are more likely to learn is that their character is going to be developed and their soul will be deeply impacted by being incarnated in real humanity. . . .

Children do not learn much when their only experience of the city is to "roll up your windows and lock your doors!" Children raised in fear become self-centered and paranoid. Instead of learning that the church is truly international and made up of people of all colors and nations, they learn to keep their distance from those who are different. Children are not stupid; they learn whom they ought to fear and whom they can trust by watching their parents. They learn who are the "good" guys and who are the "bad" guys.

Urban living is no antidote to raising fearful and self-centered children. Within the inner city they too can learn to exclude and to fear. However, exclusion in the city cannot go unnoticed. . . . Within the city, racism and conspicuous consumption are obvious. Perhaps that is the key to some of our problems. Certain environments allow lies to continue, while others force us to face them.

Principles for Raising Children in the City

You decide to commit yourselves, as a family, to the city. What now? Here are some practical points to bear in mind.

Family Ministry

God calls the whole family. If we include our children in the process of seeking God for His will for the family, it gives us the opportunity to teach children to hear God's voice. They can know for themselves that the Lord is calling them into Christian service by being part of a family in mission. Children learn from their parents. It has been our approach from our children's earliest days that they were to be a part of our ministry. God has a role for them to play.

I was thrilled when my twelve-year-old daughter came home from a camp and said to me: "Uncle Dale said that I have a destiny. He said every child in every family has a destiny. What is my destiny, Daddy?" I was excited because Misha heard what I believed deeply and had tried to model to her all of her life. God has a destiny for every child and for every family. The process of creating a sense of adventure and faith in the heart of a child is easy. When they see us asking our Father for His direction and confirmation for how our family can be a blessing to others, the enthusiasm catches.

Outward Ministry

As we raise children in the city we must teach them that they have a specific role to play in ministering to people. We taught our children how important it was to love the prostitutes and to treat them as normal human beings. We encouraged them to be friendly. This gave us the opportunity to teach our children about the dangers of paternalism, and how to respond to people when we do not agree with their lifestyles.

This whole process paid off wonderfully. One day one of our children drew a picture for a particular prostitute named Betty. Betty could not resist the temptation and came to our little home to drink coffee and ask questions about who we were. It wasn't too much later that she accepted Christ as her Savior. And it was through this experience that Misha and Matthew began to learn that God could use them as well as their mom and dad.

Spiritual Discernment

We help our children grow in discernment and maturity by dealing with the spirits of the city. We teach them the difference between cultural patterns and spiritual powers. It is important to teach our children from an early age how Satan attacks people in their minds, their bodies and their emotions.

We must teach them how to respond to such things as violence, hurriedness, impersonalness, sexual immorality, racism, economic injustice, materialism, greed and anger. These spiritual forces are at work in the city and in the hearts of the people of the city. We do this by evaluating each situation as it comes up and teaching them God's response in that situation.

Daily Living

We should teach our children practical lessons of "urban survival." This includes how to get around in the city on public transportation, how to respond to strangers, where they cannot go and when they can go and how they should behave when they are there. If we are fearful of the city they will pick up our attitudes immediately; but if we look to the Lord for His protection and His wisdom in every situation, they will develop that as an attitude of life. We must take the initiative with our children and look for those "teachable moments."

Teaching Morals

We serve our children by teaching them about modesty and purity. We allowed the questions our kids asked to set the agenda of what we taught them. What we explained to Mat-

171

thew as a five-year-old, when he asked what the prostitutes did, and what we said when he was eight years old, and then twelve years old, were all quite different.

Actually, Misha answered his question the first time! When they were five and seven years old we took them into the city to visit. We were trying to introduce them to the city in a positive way, doing fun things with them and helping them adjust to inner-city living. One night we were looking for a parking place and ended up in the red light district. Matthew saw women standing in front of windows and exclaimed from the back seat, "Look, Mommy! What are all those ladies doing without any clothes on?" Immediately Misha piped up and said, "Well, Matthew, when you do things you shouldn't do, after a while you begin to think that they are the right things to do. These ladies are breaking God's laws and now they think it is O.K. to break God's laws. If we do what is wrong, then we'll start believing it is right."

Sally was both amazed and amused at Misha's answer—amazed at her maturity and amused at how she was teaching her little brother. Later she discussed it in more depth with Matthew and Misha. That night the lesson had to do with breaking God's laws, not so much what the ladies were doing. She simply explained that they were immodest and that they did things that broke God's heart. She also explained how important it was to love them and pray for them.

Taking Time

We help our children by realizing that life takes more time in the city. The pressures of busy urban life mean kids are going to need more time for sleep. They are going to need more time with their parents. This means parents must slow down. It simply takes more time to handle all the situations and pressures that arise. It has to be worked into our schedules whether we are involved in "Christian ministry" or we have made a commitment to a neighborhood because God has called us to be there.

Practicality

We have to adjust childcare equipment and toys. We have to have strollers that fit onto buses, raingear that can fit into our bags and toys that can be used primarily inside.

Sally learned during the early days of raising our kids in the city how important it was for her to make the home a place of warmth and refreshment, a place of creativity and acceptance. Parents set the mood by their attitudes, their words and the choices they make.

Physical Exercise

It is important to provide opportunities for our children to receive proper physical exercise. Some inner-city playgrounds are adequate. There are also swimming pools, football clubs, bicycle paths, basketball courts.

Sometimes the play must be supervised. There is no reason why parents should not organize it. Talk with other concerned parents and get involved in activities with your children.

Growing in Faith

We can teach our children to trust God by giving them special faith projects. When we moved into one inner-city apartment, for example, we challenged our children (who were seven and nine at the time) to take on the challenge to pray in the finances to furnish their bedrooms. Our kids got excited about this project. They baked cookies, collected old things and sold them door to door and shared the need with their friends.

Checks came from grandparents, friends gave unexpected gifts and slowly their bank accounts mounted up. Their sense of accomplishment and trust in the Lord grew tremendously as they saw the money come in to help purchase furniture for their own rooms. They were a part of what was happening. It was a great experience for all of us.

Loving the City

It is important to help our children enjoy the city. Too often we are "in the city but not of it." Don't keep the city at a distance. Celebrate its life: Go to the theater, the concerts, the parks, the zoos, the museums; walk its streets and meet its people. Love the city and your kids will love it, too.

Time Together

It is important to have regular family times. Although Sally and I were not breakfast-eaters, we decided to make breakfast time an important family event. We both got up, helped the kids get dressed and spent time together over the breakfast table. That tradition carried on until they were teenagers.

We prayed over the day and committed our lives to the Lord. At night I helped get the children ready for bed while Sally prepared dinner. After we ate, I told them stories. I made up stories about Peter the Church Mouse, Wally the Whale and Billy Bass the Evangelist.

As the children got older we began to read good books with them. We went through *The Little House on the Prairie* series, C.S. Lewis' *Chronicles of Narnia*, J.R.R. Tolkien's *Lord of the Rings*, Kenneth Grahame's *Wind in the Willows* and many others. What a wonderful experience this was for us together as a family! It gave us many opportunities to share and talk about how things were going in their lives—and they developed a love for good literature as well.

As the kids got older, our family times became weekly, rather than daily, events. Eventually, we called family meetings as we needed them. They are still a regular part of our family life. Family meetings became a time for fun, for prayer, for personal sharing, for decision-making and for conflict resolution. It created a sense of family cohesiveness and togetherness.

Looking for the Good

We must look for God's compensations in the midst of sacrifice. There is no denying the fact that you give up something to live in some parts of the city. I learned something important about this from Sally. Early on she developed an attitude of looking for God's compensations. If she gave up something in one part of her life that was important to her, she believed the Lord would make it up in another way. I am not talking about material things. Often it would just be that the Lord would send along a friend to spend time with her, or that somebody would write a letter or that we would do something special as a family.

The most important part of this attitude was the fact that Sally went through life looking for God's goodness in the little and big things of life. She has passed this attitude on to me and to our children, and it has been a wonderful blessing to us all.

A Listening Ear

There is no substitute for listening to our children. I realized early on in my life that we needed to do things together that would allow me to hear the hearts of my kids. I believed strongly that if they were to enter into my world, I first needed to enter their world. I believed I was to create a bridge through friendship that would allow them to know they could talk to me or to Sally anytime they wanted.

Matthew and I often played pool together. We also developed a passion for video games. Misha and I have often gone to movies, to a museum or out for a drink of hot chocolate. Sally does the same thing with the kids regularly, having special times with each of them.

These are times to listen to our children. Often the parents speak and the children listen. But we need to learn to reverse this role and become active listeners. This shows that we consider our children important and that we respect their feelings and emotions.

We have always encouraged our kids to share honestly with us their feelings, taking them seriously and letting them know that whatever they feel, we accept them. I believe it is important to show them by our attitude they can be honest with us and with God.

Constant in Prayer

We tried to teach our children dependence upon the Lord by praying about everything that happened in our lives. I believe it is extremely important to give our kids an opportunity to share their emotions with us honestly, but then we must go beyond that to telling God how we feel. By praying together with our children and encouraging them to express their hearts to God, we teach them that God is trustworthy, that He is accepting, that He is patient and that He has time for them.

And when the answers come to their prayers, they learn that God is involved in their lives. We have to teach them, obviously, that He often answers in ways we do not expect or that we do not like as well.

Family Hospitality

We must teach our children the blessings of hospitality. Whether we foster children and take them into our homes, invite strangers in for a meal or spend time with our friends, hospitality shows where our priorities are. People take precedence over projects and programs.

We should include our kids in family hospitality. They can participate in the process of preparing as well as cleaning up meals. Sharing around the meal table with guests and enjoying the people God brings into our home is a great opportunity to learn.

Several years ago a really wonderful woman of God singled Matthew out after a meal together in our home and spent hours with him. She shared experiences from her life, and then listened to him as he told about things he enjoyed doing.

It was an unexpected fruit of the hospitality of our home and it meant a lot to us and to Matthew.

Some years ago our friends Jim and Rona Gilchrist moved into Otara, a part of Auckland, New Zealand. Auckland is actually the largest Polynesian city in the world. More island people live in Auckland than any other one city, including the island nations of the South Pacific.

They were surrounded by gangs of Tongans, Samoans and other island youth. The night they moved into the neighborhood there was a gang fight on the street in front of them. One gang tried to burn down a house of another gang. Two nights later there was an attempted rape two doors down from them. Right after that there was a murder four doors away.

Jim and Rona felt the Lord had called them to that neighborhood to be involved in the lives of those young men and women. Over the years they have taken in almost one hundred people—as many as twenty-five at a time.

Has this affected their own three children? Yes, but not negatively. They all love the Lord all the more for Jim and Rona's commitment to get involved with the young people in their city and neighborhood.

Your family may not be called to live in a red light district or to take in gang kids, but every family is called. The calling is for you to discover, but a calling it is.

By committing ourselves to a lifestyle of service in the city to which God leads us, we not only bring great joy to the heart of our Father in heaven; we also embark on a journey of pain and glory, one that will challenge us and, more important, change us.

It is never too late to start the journey.

Bibliography

Bakke, Ray. *The Urban Christian*. Downers Grove, Ill.: InterVarsity Press, 1987.

Barrett, David. *World-Class Cities and World Evangelization*. Birmingham, Ala.: New Hope, 1988.

Calling Our Cities to Christ. Nutley, N.J.: Presbyterian and Reformed Publishing Co., 1974.

Conn, Harvie. *A Clarified Vision for Urban Mission*. Grand Rapids, Mich.: Zondervan Publishing House, 1987.

Dawson, John. *Taking Our Cities for God*. Lake Mary, Fla.: Creation House, 1989.

Greenway, Roger. *Apostles to the City*. Grand Rapids, Mich.: Baker Book House, 1978.

———. *Cities: Missions New Fontier*. Grand Rapids, Mich.: Baker Book House, 1989.

———. *Guidelines for Urban Church Planting*. Grand Rapids, Mich.: Baker Book House, 1976.

Hadaway, Rose. *The Urban Challenge*. Nashville, Tenn.: Broadman Press, 1982.

Ludwig, Charles. *Cities in New Testament Times*. Denver, Col.: Accent Books, 1976.

McClung, Floyd and Kalafi Moala. *Nine Worlds to Win*. Word U.K., 1990.

Torney, George. *Toward Creative Urban Strategy*. Irving, Tex.: Word Books, 1970.